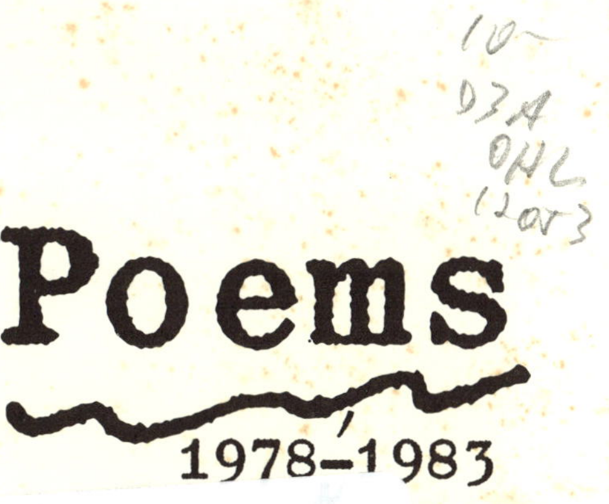

Poems
1978–1983

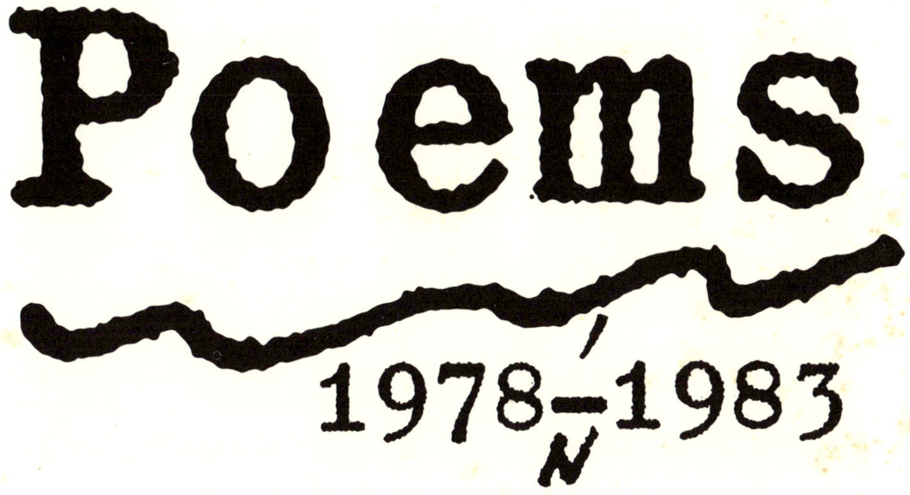

Poems 1978–1983

Edited by **Robert Fox**,
Writer in Residence

Aid to Individual Artists Fellowship
Program/**Creative Writing**
Ohio Arts Council

Ohio Arts Council
727 East Main Street
Columbus, Ohio 43205-1796
telephone 614/466-2613

Published by Ohio Designer Craftsmen
for the Ohio Arts Council
727 East Main Street
Columbus, Ohio 43205-1796

Design & Illustration:
Micheal Milligan, Design Arts Coordinator & Graphic Designer
Editorial Production:
Laura Wallencheck, Public Information Specialist
Design Assistance:
Ellen Hoover, Assistant Graphic Designer

Library of Congress Cataloging in Publication Data
Main entry under title:

Poems, 1978-83.

   Poems by recipients of the Ohio Arts Council's Aid
to Individual Artists Fellowship Program/Creative
Writing.
   Includes bibliographical references.
   1. American poetry—Ohio. 2. American poetry—20th
century. I. Fox, Robert, 1943-   . II. Ohio Arts
Council.
PS571.03P6   1983   811'.54'0809771   83-13163
ISBN 0-913335-00-2

Printed in the United States of America

1 2 3 4 5 6 7 8 9 10 — 89 88 87 86 85 84 83

Contents

About the OAC

I am pleased to say thank you to John Henle, former chairman of the Ohio Arts
Council, who has been a longtime supporter of individual artists in this state, and
to my sensitive staff who are responsible for publications of this kind. Staff members
such as Denny Griffith, Bob Fox, Micheal Milligan and Laura Wallencheck are
working artists who have contributed their talents and energies to make this
anthology an imaginative one. They are supported, in turn, by a very good state
arts council and a very generous legislature.

Ohio's individual artists give much to Ohio by generating an exciting atmosphere
in which to live. This book is but one demonstration of their creativity.

Wayne P. Lawson, Ph.D.
Executive Director

About the Program

The Ohio Arts Council began awarding grants to Ohio writers in 1978 with the
inception of the Aid to Individual Artists Program. Ohio's support for its artists is
fairly well known; with one of the largest fellowship programs of any state in the
country, direct grant awards to writers in support of the creation of new works
have helped to sustain and encourage one of the most active literary communities
in the nation.

From 1978 through 1983, eighty-nine individuals received grant awards in the
writers' category. This list includes recipients who work in poetry, fiction, non-fiction,
criticism and playwriting. The OAC awards funds by considering only the quality
of the writing submitted rather than the nature of the project proposal; in short,
strong writing wins out over the ability to craft a jazzy proposal. Grant application
materials are reviewed by professional peers. Panel members both in-state and out-
of-state consider writers' submissions in light of the strength and relative merits of
the work, and as an advisory body pass along their recommendations for funding
to the Council for final approval.

This anthology contains poems by both fellowship recipients (who have received
grant awards of up to $6,000) and mini-grant recipients (up to $500). In recogni-
tion that many writers have more than one strong suit, grantees from all writing
categories were invited to submit. The following selections represent those writers
who responded.

Plans for a followup anthology of prose (fiction and non-fiction) are underway
for 1984.

Denny Griffith
Previous Coordinator, Aid to Individual Artists Program

About the Writers

Many of you might not know that there are over two hundred serious writers
in Ohio who produce high-quality fiction, non-fiction, criticism, poetry and drama.
With each year's arrival of Individual Artists grant applications come revelations.
The variety is as refreshing as the quality, and all styles are represented. Ohio
stands out as a microcosm of the literary ferment occurring across the country; it
is also evolving into a very special geographical locality, given a new definition
by its writers.

While some of the following voices have been around for some time, and while
some fellowship winners included here no longer reside in the state, collectively
the poems represent a heretofore undiscovered major Ohio resource, a great
literary richness.

Editing this collection has recreated for me the excitement of some of my discoveries
over the last five years, the talent recognized by the various fellowship panels. I hope
you will share the excitement of the poems themselves.

The appendix contains biographical and bibliographical information about the writers.

Robert Fox
Writer in Residence

While Waiting for a Friend to Come to Visit a Friend in a Mental Hospital/Russell Atkins

eyes thieve with prickled stir:
the attendant has ideas about me

the attendant keeps watch, watching
that abrupt wild uranium grow a bat's ears,
sardine flowers, moons' eggs,
                    stomach guitars,
a double-bass rump—but he's err:
one shrewds to his inferences,
here where the world's sharp'd
sheen'd across with antiseptic spear

always be afar if it is challenge,
the off-shores of the eyes direct
devilishly in this "catch me" business

I have about the least to do
with white-coated attendants,
              soft'd thither nurses,
and the sleep particles—

stop looking
        (—a friend's gone banking
and I'm waiting
        that is all

Football Practice in Woodland Haven/Russell Atkins

it is year's whir to late:
the unsandblasted Jesuses
      the iron angels beaten blue to a tarnish
seen severally between the forward passes
to receivers or a fielded kickoff
a twenty-yard line of exuberance—
the team of boys has taken over
      with its line of scrimmage

(through all that's orotund of sacristy
the appalled ministers have not spoken:
kids play the game and rock the graves

Who does complain? stark old Schaferhaus?
(he'd offer them participation)
fans in the boxes pull on their shrouds
and the shaken skulls glee together
in damp stands, all teeth, are all of cheer

one hour again out of dark perpetuity

Lakefront, Cleveland/Russell Atkins

The stretch outcast night's long'd:
a hideous voyage of far
under'd sepulchral sky
colossal as a grave's after I
stood by monuments of thrust rocks
shouldered together that tremendous'd,
vaulted and rent themselves over sea
There was extremed
dark of the city

(a woman somewhere having secreted her burden
          cast in a toilet
  a jellied fetus
    —a surgeon's blade hysterically sharp)

waves slid away
a murmur of laps
  —there lo! I saw
it   pulp

as stretch outcast the night,
and hideous voyage of far
under'd sepulchral sky
colossal as a grave's after
this pulp came down
the dark city—!

listen: I'd swear
I heard, heard low
its sigh-sounds lapse
as from furious determination—
furious, horrid determination!
Though stretch outcast the night,
though hideous voyaged afar,
though there was extremed
back of the city,
though there's excruciation
under sepulchral sky,
though there is grave's after
and grave's before, I heard
I swear, some of furious determination—
heard go the sigh
before I swept it to muck
with a laugh of cry!

No Matter/John M. Bennett

He was locked in the parkinglot behind
gates of high bent wire he sat in the gravel
looked at the bottom of his pants his
cracking shoes and hands dangling between his legs

I was stumbling down the hall I was
seeing lurching shadows where the wall should be
I was starting to see the door I was
jumping back I was
waking up and shaking there

I'll be crouching in a doorway,
soldiers running past, a fire up the block
I hold my legs I clamp my eyes between my knees a
silence gapes up over gunshots far away
I'll start to move I'll
see a priest run screaming down the street
leaping through the flames

He sat in his car and slept and dreamed one word over and
over, said it into his own drumming ears, he's
standing before a grey evenwaved sea MATTER
MATTER MATTER the traffic sucking and rocking in the
street outside the fence

The Woman Who Collaborates /James Bertolino

There is a woman who collaborates
with the sun. She is water,
she's fire. She makes the melon ripen
and the squash blossoms flower.

There is a woman who collaborates
with the tides—every mollusk
wakens to her name. Every kelp string and weed
swims to her breathing.

There is a woman who collaborates with air,
who brings the ancient forests to flame.
She laughs and mountains explode.
She hums and the earth shudders open.

There is a woman who collaborates
with our dream. Our long fears love her,
and she is the leader, she is to blame.

Beware the Roses/James Bertolino

<u>For Anselm Parlatore</u>

Sure, I'm in a state
of mental health. Of course I am.
but that doesn't mean I don't see
the little tricks the organizers play on us.
Just because the foxglove and the rose
have the same bloody pink, I'm not fooled,
I can hear the noise. Can't you?
Can't you almost feel them thinking envy
for your feet, your fingers? The roses, I mean.
Don't worry about the foxglove. Why just
this morning a tiny rosebud, no bigger than
a roach's folded wings, demanded I stop breathing
near her. She claimed my breath would cause her blight.
I knew she wished to bring confusion
to my system, so I reached out
my slender fingers and
broke her stem.

The Cocoon /James Bertolino

Time still passes unevenly.

Now a streaky pocket,
now a stuttering
dissipation—
our cosmos resembles
an Asian's dream of fresh eggs.

A black phone rings in the garden.

Somehow the wooly morning
breaks into autumn,
subtle region
where memory colors the maple leaf.

A golden garden spider is spinning
the moth's second cocoon.

We are constituted.
We are the fully cleared.

Love brings the old chair.

Under the Covers/Laurel Blossom

Certain nights
When the pillow fit just right under my neck,
When the flashlight tucked under my arm stayed tucked,
The novel on my knees stayed propped up
And my parents had somebody over,

When the world was well-bred
And the heroine was young, and the moon hung yellow
And perfectly round on the page that explained
What everything meant:

Then it was heaven on the second floor,
In the corner bedroom, in the one twin bed,
Under the bedspread and the blankets and the pure
One hundred percent cotton sheet

Made in this country before the war.
Plots thickened. They don't do that anymore.
Characters lived. In the ventilated air
Their voices could almost be heard
Downstairs, talking things over.

Leaving/Laurel Blossom

Oblivious.
That's one way. To blot him out.
Others include the years you keep packed for
Morocco, the first chance, the next
train, or some sudden death
in the family: my grandmother used to say
<u>murder yes, divorce never.</u>
My grandfather nodded at her wake.
That's another.

A girl goes with her mother. Example:
say it's spring out, it's no fair,
say he stands there, calling you <u>pumpkin.</u>
Handsomer than you thought,
but not that handsome. Your father
has something to tell you, she tells you.
Information about traps and doors

you're never going to need, not ever.

As to the others, estimates
vary: some say the rest of our lives.
My friend H says a person
is here or not here. H is divorced,
she has two children. She loves her life
<u>any minute.</u> I'm not making fun.
Since from the first, from here
on in, these are choices:
our mothers did not make them for us.

Habit-forming /Laurel Blossom

Before you know you know it
the way it goes
something like this, for instance
something to do with April
Monday: before you know it
you, in your skin
touching mine.

Four days straight: it was easy.
I didn't think about this
cold-turkey
beached, out of cigarettes

summer and so on

Unexposed /Phil Boiarski

Roofline,
Tree trunk,
Evergreen
Shadows
Shape the frost
By shielding the sun.

Their pale
Shadows, hard-edged
Hoary silhouettes
Struck in light,
Framed by the dark
Lawn of glistening blades.

Where the serous ice
Emerges into dew,
Light cuts out
Negatives.

Secrets /Phil Boiarski

Such is the subtle power
Sinners tender their confessors
That they never forgive them
For knowing.

Sworn to keep so many secrets
Like a cache of cluster bombs
Hidden in the Holy City,
Or a poisoned <u>pomme</u>.

It is not my fault.
I knelt at the foot
Of the altar and
Struck my breast.

I know they want my testimony
Against them. I know they
Want to be caught
And forgiven.

One whisper, like clouded
Cubes melting in a tepid drink,
And it would be clear as water.

My tongue, loosened, worms out
Like a winter snake, warming
To the thaw. I fight
To keep it clenched
In my jaw.

Ohio Spring Storm /Imogene L. Bolls

Somewhere someone is losing a roof,
shingles ripped away like years of a life
carefully planned, chimneys tumbling;
or a barn's red sides folding
out from under golden haymows.
The sky is the same pea-gray-green
I remember from Kansas, how
tornadoes come in technicolor across
the big screen, in spite of Metro-Goldwyn
Mayer and Oz and Dorothy. Somewhere
the rending wind decorates ground
with an upturned couch (maroon), a blue blanket,
or, in Xenia, a toy pink rabbit
stuffed in the guttering of a sucked-out house.
Above us clouds roil, stampede down
the sky all hoofs and gray dust.
Green pliable trees lean out of the way
as we brace for wind. But being in
neither the time nor the place,
we get only a little rain.

The Dream/Imogene L. Bolls

This is the place I was not ready
to leave.

I lifted my feet, lighter and lighter,
up the mountain,

up where a buck in velvet hung
curious in aspen,

up where a red-tailed hawk lifted
and caught wind.

I walked until my thoughts became
like clouds.

I rested among paintbrush and lupine
and penstemon.

Far off people shouted, calling
my name.

I called back, but my mouth
let no sound.

Through high ponderosa only
the wind came.

Deer Watching in Frijoles Canyon/Imogene L. Bolls

They live on the edge of meadows and hunger
and escape. Tensed with adrenalin, hushed
in seclusion of rabbitbrush and willows
they stand like bone china ready

to break at a footfall. Moving off
they turn to browse on willow leaves,
letting their long legs lock
and unlock at the knees, placing
each foot carefully ahead

in the cool grass. As if walking
on glass they drift away from intrusion,
like the heart, steady, but ready
to break at one miscalculation.

In Retrospect: Oedipus to the Sphinx /Imogene L. Bolls

Winged woman with lion thighs,
voluptuous on hairy haunches,
curling glutted smiles back
upon lunches of fouled flesh—
Shrew, I will unriddle you.
It was in childhood I crawled
from the crib of my curse,
my feet bound and pierced,
and was saved for suffering
by one whose excuse
was humanity. In manhood,
it was in fear and shame
my two strong legs bore me
faster than prophecy,
with an arrow's aim,
to the crossroads of doom.
Alas, with age I walk upon
three legs away from Thebes
(a rain of blood upon my life),
leaning my blinding wisdom
on a cane of grief.

Responsibilities/Grace Butcher

Across the melting ice and snow
great gray dogs run at me
because I also run. They think
this is their wilderness. I must
prove them wrong. I am ready,
warm and happy, to kill them
as they leap at me.

Also the earth for some reason
pounds at my feet. Yes, I suppose
to have a love like this, I must be
punished somehow, or made to
appreciate the earth more by its
hurting me this way. Whose logic is this?
What is all this pain about?

All this sacrifice of animals and all
this pain I offer up each year to make
the summer come and oil my skin with sweat—
maybe it would come without all this.
But I am afraid to think what would happen
to this earth without me. My running is necessary.
It keeps things the way they are.

New and Old Beginnings /Grace Butcher

At the end of the poem is the white space,
like moving out into a vast field at twilight
with snow falling over snow already fallen,
and feeling the beginning of fear
as if perhaps this time the path will lead nowhere,
or is not even to be found at all. What then?
Here at the edge, at least my own footprints
are familiar. A cold wind moves the darkness
around. I grow dark with the darkening air,
but wait for a sign.
                    In the distance, a light.
It may be the farm of some people who are dead now.
I wonder if they will remember me? (As if walking
across this vastness would change anything!)
The light seems to come and go in the wind.
It is probably as good a sign as any.
Suddenly eager, I start across the field,
my feet making whispering sounds in the snow.
I realize I am walking in an old straight furrow;
I can not see it in the swirling darkness,
but it will take me anywhere I need to go.

Day Full of Rustling Murmuring Lies /Grace Butcher

I can't hear you in the wind.
Don't come on a windy day;
come in silence.
All day the wind blows;
sounds are not real.
The wind walks in the grass,
drives down the road,
and it is never you.
Even though I wait with all my senses,
nothing I perceive is ever you
on days like this.
Doors open and slam,
windows tremble, a dead limb
cracks and falls.
I jump at the sounds;
movement is always catching my eye.
It is never anyone.

Come in the still twilight
or in the quiet morning before the sun.
Walk on the sidewalk loudly with your boots.
Whistle something familiar.
Say my name in your own voice.
Do anything that the wind does not do
so   I know it is you.
The wind is never true.

Wife of the Moon Man Who Never Came Back

/Grace Butcher

Often when the moon is full
they have to give her something
to make her sleep.
She confuses "moon" with "mine"
and has been known
to run naked on the lawn
screaming his name
and singing children's songs.
The familiar face
terrifies her.

Certain nights
she opens the curtains,
the windows,
opens her thighs,
her darkest places.
His body, thin silver now,
pours into her with no warmth;
her fingers crawl like animals
to their dark hole.

Thrilled and horrified,
she breathes the rush of silver air
with lungs that grow thick.
It is a familiar feeling:
the dust falling on her open eyes,
shadows or someone screaming,
caught in the surge of gigantic tides.

Hospital Visit /Anne Chamberlain

"Can I do anything?" You shake your head
and smile, the words unsaid
drift pale as mist
and fade into the air,
you lying there.
"Can I help in any way?" The pain
between us moving,
sharp beyond disguise,
deep in your eyes
the mute and desperate loving,
the faint call
through miles of loneliness
to me. To all.
"They tell me I must leave." But we are gone
on a swift flight together, hand in hand,
from sterile walls
through bleak and haunted halls
past time and memory to the sweet land
of love more strong than anguish
and more dear
than all the joys denied you
and more clear
than morning at its lightest
and more brave
than the flesh we cherish,
and we cannot save.
"I will be back soon." You understand,
We wing forever in the quiet land.

The Wolf/Hale Chatfield

I: The Wolf Expresses His Intention of Retelling an Old Tale

"More's the pity," she used to say
"More's the pity."
My own grandmother.
Keen in her sense of what was shame,
what was pitiful, she was purblind
to catastrophe.
          That I should feel the need
to tell this hackneyed tale
is tragedy enough
that she would fail to feel it.

More's the pity.
Herself a wolf.
Herself a tragedy.
Thus to my own grandmother
I dedicate this catastrophe—
this cliche:
       a girl's story
told from such an unexpected
point of view
as to be predictable—
as inevitable as that the story of a fright
be told by thunder,
effect by cause,
Saturday by Friday night,
man by handle,
by me a girl unmourned,
reap by sow,
flowerbed by Vigoro
        (more's the pity)
by Grandmother Grandembryo.

II: The Wolf Imagines the Girl in Red Singing to Him in the Wood

Wolf.
Bad cause, invariable villain.
My dear loser.

See how I take
delicious shape from your worst
thoughts, how I burst
from your hiding place
sudden and clean as a shower,
and am innocence.

See how from your lair
I unbed myself like a flower
uprooted and spring
forth into the green valleys,
lilting and tripping,
from your covert silence
swell into song.

Oh wolf.
Oh terrible eyes.

See how I slip forth
like a lily into the light.

Oh monster.
Oh you longing mouth.

See how I am like
golden hair let down in darkness,
untied ribbon,
a flow of cloth.

Wolf.
You hunger.
You knot and cluster of need.

See how I am yourself
set free as a vapor among stars.

Your silver rib
shaped to a tuning fork,
and touched.

A melody.

Your own song.

III: The Wolf Soliloquizes Concerning His Lamentable Condition

If in the
valley of shades
some form follows
or awaits some function
in this instance it is I.
I hide.

I seek to leap from my own shadows
and molest myself.

A fleeting glimpse.

The red sheen
of a cloak caught in my eye's corner
paining me. The skitter of dainty feet
a light in my terrible darkness.

I waylay my innocence
in fitfalls of good deeds.

I am a mugger
in a dark mirror.

A good woods.

**IV: The Wolf, Reluctant to Rehearse the Entire Series of Events,
    Elects Instead to Sing the Blues**

Truth to tell,
I'd had a bitter night,
and I awoke uneasy
and alone.

There was a dark, unlikely morning.
There was a silence like the din of horns.
There was a most unnatural despair.
There was myself.

And I gathered up myself
and all the fragments of that awesome
solitude into a choke
as hard and sour as a mouthful
of unripened apple,
and I sought to sob,
to come undone.
> Truth to tell,
> I'd hoped to weep.
> I'd hoped to gentle me,
> unravel, and be kind.

I'd hoped to see
a way, but if a way was there,
then I was blind—
all pulled up into my mind
and knotted there
like a ball of hair
and skin and bone
excreted by an owl.

> Truth to tell,
> no one had heard of her;
> less I.

I'd never hoped to see
her; not see
her die.

But I had had a bitter night,
and thus, in my despair,
imagine how surprised (and glad!) I was
to see her there—

unbidden,
unimagined,
unendangered. There.

I was a wolf for all of that.
And she had eyes.

All golden, and an instant light,
she saw me and she fled:

red was her sudden absence
in my sight as if I'd bled
her image into my own eye
and had believed my blood.

Red Ridinghood.
Red Ridinghood.

Short Story /Sister Maryanna Childs, O.P.

He spoke straightforward iambic tetrameter;
She fluted mostly dactyllic hexameter.
He was a single metaphor, a rock;
She had as many similes as a flock
Of orioles, a garden full of bloom.
Their glances met one day across a room:
A bird may light upon a rock, a rose wreathe
                round it.
"It will not work," the critics said and yet
                they found it
Successful in all seasons, every weather.

Their children spoke a different language
                altogether.

The Wise Cow's Tale /Sister Maryanna Childs, O.P.

As they say in Galway:
> An Irish cow is a horse of another color.

They looked so gentle, grazing by Lough Derg, that I
Sidled up to a brown cow and looked her in the eye.
"How now, brown cow," said I facetiously;
She flicked her eyelashes disdainfully.
"Let's keep this on an intellectual plane," said she.
"Don't you know we Irish cows are wiser than thine?
A little less than kin, but more than kine!
Ever since medieval days, when the tough hide
That held us cows together became the pride
Of monks who copied the Scriptures prayerfully,
Binding them in our cowhide carefully.
Did you never hear of the <u>Book of the Dun Cow</u>?
Did you not? She was an ancestor, now.
My mother told me the story long ago.
"Oh," she switched her tail, "and did you know
That Saint Columba once illegally
Copied the <u>Book of Psalms</u> Saint Finnian lent him, secretly?
There was a court case," the brown cow tossed her head,
"And do you know what the Judge, the High King, said?
'To every cow her calf and to every book its copy,' a just decree,
As even good Saint Columba had to agree.
And later, when the Hedge Schoolmasters came
Into the barns to keep alive Learning's flame,
They taught the young lads Virgil and Homer and they in turn
Repeated the Latin and Greek to us and all did learn.
So be off with your how-now and your
> cow-that-jumped-over-the-moon
And brush up on our Irish History, aroon."

Sister Mary Appassionata Lectures the Religion and Mythology Classes: Frogs and Foreskins, Heart and Tongue

/David Citino

A frog from Egypt's plague, piece of reed
from baby Moses' yacht. Two lumps of lard—
what's left of Lawrence and Joan. A piece
of Shadrach's unsinged robe. Pine shavings
curlicued from Joseph's plane, sawdust
from his rasp, divine chips off
the old block. The Bambino's foreskin.
Feathers from Noah's dove, droppings from
the one that blessed the Apostles' tongues,
the raucous jay Francis shut up with his
simple singing. Feathers from
the engendering wings of Gabriel.
Wormy core of Adam's unswallowable apple.
Comb from the cock that crowed to reproach
Peter. Bones from Balaam's
eloquent ass. Feet of four and twenty crows
knocked out of the sky by Loreto's
high-flying house. Pickled in a canning jar:
Lucy's most discerning eyes, Agatha's nipples,
the herring bone Blaise made the boy cough up,
whole and unaltered hymens of Veronica
and Mary, Holofernes' ear, Cecilia's
vocal cords, heart and tongue of Isaac Jogues,
Abel's skull, irreparably shattered.
A quart of milk from Mary's right breast.

We can't be damned for not believing in these;
only for being so cocksure this world's
a place narrow as the space between our own
eyes and ears, death's-head cell of darkness and bone,
hell of thinking always only that we know.

Sister Mary Appassionata Lectures the Neurology Class
/David Citino

If woman and man are willful, mindful hunks
of tissue, blood and bone what is it wills, minds

them? If they're wills and minds embodied to make them
real enough to move to love what is it embodies them?

For two years Soviet scientists with stainless blades
sliced up Lenin's brain, yet learned nothing about

learning. Technicians splattered Walt Whitman's
brain on the laboratory floor and tried to claim

it was an accident. Is knowledge the last supper?
Worms learn tricks by feasting on worms who've already

learned. So do we cannibalize our past. The flash
of light erupting in the neural cell bright as

Venus rising or stars falling from heaven rescues us
from caves of skull, root and bark of limbs, blazes

into thought, a gift of fire, we think, we know.

Thomas Alva Edison Writes to Madame Elena Blavatsky, 1878 /David Citino

Knowing? It's memory, my dear teacher, coming
from rarer worlds than ours, swarming through
eye and ear, between lips, ideas like light
streaming into stained windows of the cathedral

of skull. A lifetime's the dropcloth of memory,
my wisdom. Age? A blow to the head, crushed
egg shell. The great amnesia. Memory oozes out
to seek new hosts, indelible, flammable as

oil. All last night, love, I sat in the lab,
electric coil wound around my head like
bandages, trying to invent what others hear,
think, feel: a telepathy of love. Nothing

came of it. But I know we're electric, body
and soul, my creativity, every thought or pain
a fire real as the disembodied voice in the ear,
melodies spinning from every nowhere, figures dancing

on the wall, light at once where darkness ruled.

Cloudbank/Marian Clover

Lulled, we fly through evolutions.
Perched on the edge of a frothing volcano,
we dip into caves of brute fluff.
Beneath a whirlpool, coral collects.
Giant clams convene. Gnomes and dwarfs
look down on me. I watch a dragon being
born, race past a menace of mastodons.
Even here is waste, heaps of uncaged
ribs and skulls.
Flimsy and tough, some clouds stand alone,
curlicued trees, trunks leaking white roots,
turning to jellyfish, tentacles swaying.
Propped on snarling spines, our cargo
of jokes and history stored in the luggage bay,
we share nothing but restraint.
Lighted words flick us alert, the squawk
commanding us to truss ourselves, and
the ship noses down between cotton bolls,
descending to blue splashed from a paintbox.
Down so low we see the links. Roads connected
to rivers swelling to harbors thinning to streams
joined to oceans. All of the earth laced together
by water, with new light at all the edges.

Craftsman/Marian Clover

Muttering Swedish oaths at the reluctant wood,
your unequal adversary, I watched you carve
what-not shelves out of lumber, hack benches
out of boards. Fondling corners, stroking
the grain, loving the plumb line, the arc,
planes and angles and the rare perfect corner.

Now your tools lie idle. I watch you pick
at starched conversation, checking the corners,
the planes and angles of the only pane of light
that's left from your slab of bed.

And I am jealous still, of scraps of wood.

Architecture/Marian Clover

People loom like buildings on the seascape,
hunched against a horizon that curves
the rigid house of bone.
I see squatting mosques, a lanky skyscraper
wearing a navel, a tottering Roman villa,
clusters of Stonehenge spines, and
one brash row of teepees in the act of folding.

How I Know It's Over:

/Horace Coleman

breathing on the winter window
is just like kissing you.
the warmth fades so quickly
a lonely chill elevators down my spine.

/Horace Coleman

at
Pemaquid Point
light house
the pines lean
down to the sea
the sea comes up to the rocks
the rocks rock in between

No Sweat Vet /Horace Coleman

I accepted my lot—
when they sent me I fought.
Yes, I killed; but I also saved.
While I was gone some chanted
—when I came home some raved.
While in my wild dreams
I sweated and panted.

Did I do more wrong
than the Viet Cong?
What you think you see isn't me
—it's just the shadow
of what you fear you might be.
You can let the mirror drop
but the reflection won't stop.

The war was sweeter
        than the peace
but I'm a survivor
        who found release.
The rotting bitterness didn't
        go too far—
I know I'm at least
        a Bronze Star

when a hero is a zero
the land cannot stand

Danny's Uncle/Wayne Dodd

All the rest of it I remember
perfectly, even the four o'clocks and peonies
in the yard of the black captain of detectives
across the street, the first one
in our block. And the lush smell of panties
the racecar driver's girlfriend left behind
next door, tossed playfully into our faces now
at dusk, the heat of August
and puberty already driving us steadily
out of our minds. Sometimes,
that summer, alone
in the house, I secretly shot pigeons
off our landlady's roof
with a .22. They fell,
I supposed, into bushes underneath bedroom
windows, soft and smooth
as her daughter's new breasts.
Or perhaps they suffered only
broken wings and walked unsteadily off
into the fractured world
of 5th Street, like suicide notes
scattering in the dark.
One evening, I remember,
through the heavy smell of food drifting
out of windows, I came home and found
for supper
my mother screaming
she wanted to die. There
in the kitchen my father's face
was like the broken sidewalk in front of our house.

Yes we do love you, we screamed, among the pots,
among the ladles, We do, we love you,
until at last she laid her head
down in the empty plate before her
and clutched the small table
tight in both her outstretched arms.
But him I can't remember
at all, only the photograph, large
and glossy on the living room wall,
the sleek body poised and glistening
in the ring, the raised fists dark
messages in the failing light.

Of Butterflies/Wayne Dodd

There can be no doubt, the same
one, come back for the ninth
day in a row to the boards
beside me: the small tear
in the wing tip, the curved
line in the opened
wings, like a horseshoe's brown
shape stamped strangely
on the earth, antennae
sifting the air
for messages.

What is it that brings it
always back
to this spot
and me? like an image
of my mother, standing small
and bright in the summer
grass, raising her arms
from the shoulders
of the light voile dress my
father gave her
on her birthday . . .

You walk down a familiar road one day
in August, the sun setting
behind you, the light wind cooling your chest
and arms. The trees are beginning to give up
the light they held all day
in their leaves, and cicadas rasp to a stop
along the branches.
Then, for an instant,
on top of a fence post
a man you've never seen
before appears, soft hat pushed
back from his forehead,
one leg swinging
down, arm raised
in greeting.
And as you sit
to supper,
a bluebird, in the last
clarity of light outside,
darts again and
again against the window.
Thus young men pack their bags
one morning and catch a train
to a city they've never been to,
or else walk off
with only change in their pockets,
certain they will find, in a bed
somewhere a brother, withdrawing
in fever,
his thin hand fluttering
in final recognition.

We Knew the Signs/Leatrice W. Emeruwa

4:50 p.m.

Mama loomed large
as a Bengal tiger
in her brown striped housedresses
when we were small. Stood tall
and strong and fierce.
All-knowing.
High cheekbones flanked
roman nose and dark eyes
snapped e-s-p messages
when we dared to tightrope
her patience.
Tough she had never seen
nor read about the South Sea isles,
wild black natural hair framed
her face Fiji-style.
I usta think, "Mama,
is you an Injun
with frizzy hair?"
Some days she'd go about
with thin lips clenched tight.
Held back ancestral anguish.
We knew the signs.
Half-asleep we'd hear
the water sounds and tiptoe steps
of papa's leaving early
before sun-up darkness.

He'd come back late, late at night
Mama always met him at the bolted Kitchen door
and we strained to hear
his raspy "Nothin'!"
Then papa'd stamp into the hall closet.
Rummage out his pawn shop-church-and funeral suit
and slam the house.
Return with our evening meal.
While mama fried the salt pork,
warmed the syrup and baked the hoecakes
on top the pot-bellied stove;
papa sat like Red Mountain
his face a silent scream
and worried the borrowed want-ads.
Lil Bruh and I knew to
whisper our finger games.
But the shadow-children
of the coal-oil lamp played hide-and-seek
around the kitchen walls.
We knew the signs.

The Jesus Lady /Leatrice W. Emeruwa

Where is she now? I wonder.

The Jesus lady who harassed passers-bye
      swore Jehovah sent her to stand
      Gabriel-like at Second and Euclid
      offering salvation to all
      with time enough to spare.

Though I never stopped for sidewalk grace
I found her most intriguing of those
peddlers sanctifying downtown's space:
Pleasant, round face, indeterminate age, neatly
uniformed in white. I wonder whose she is:
wife? mother? sister? daughter? dark angel?

For two summers she would
at that same spot flail her tambourine about
use bullhorn to holler out in stentorian voice:
"Ya betta get your soul saved now!"

She intimidated the very air.
Some who hurried by hid their eyes
as though they feared heaven then and there.
"Ya betta listen to me," she'd shout.
"Jeeezus! Jeee-zus!"

She has not been seen this summer nor last.
Perhaps she moved on. . . .
      found other city streets
      found other willing souls. I wonder.

From Here /Barbara Fialkowski

<u>for D.</u>

i.

Our tongues swell
with the unspoken, anger
rising in welts from self-
flagellation—the stigmata
of silence. Thirty
some years and they
have not gotten a sound
from us yet.

Outside, the winds
move the hedges in uncertain
violence. Everything
is twig and bough,
the bare bones
of January.

ii.

Our children
feed their rabbits
imaginary carrots,
or their imaginary
rabbits, real carrots.
They know it does not
matter one way
or the other.
What we have lost,
this severing,
this decision to be
adult in all matters.

And we refuse
to cater to anything
having catered to everything
too long, only now,
bereft or star and ship,
the moon's merely a scar,
a hieroglyph for screaming.
The letter "C"
has been eclipsed
in the usual way.

iii.

Our friends have moved
into the house next door
to their house. <u>The move's
the thing</u>. We've tried
staying, tried dealing
with carpenters as if
they could make us over,
abandoned last fall,
left us splintered
edges of wood, unpapered
walls, left us helpless.
Where to begin, sent
them off not thinking
we'd have to do it
ourselves.

And our books—
books, books, books—
yours, the 18th century,
a grim jail of rationalism,
a formalism we've clung
to like the rock
of ages, or mine,
<u>Heart's Needle, The Dream
Songs</u>, those borrowings
from others in defence
of our own paralysis.
We have all slept
slumped over our books.
What have we done
with it, where
has it gone?

iv.

Upstairs, our children
sing, <u>read to us</u>,
and we delay knowing—
their closeness
too real for words,
overwhelmed,
moved to tears.

And they become
afraid as we were,
as we do, and we hug
them unto death.

v.

Retreat is the best
decision, my friend.
You're the first
to move, to descend
the long stairway
down to where
the oxygen diminishes,
descending as if my
own heart sent out
before me, no messenger,
but a deer, halting
and nervous at the
clearing.

Test the air
for the hunter's
scent, for the ring
of the rifle's
suicide, for the last
red touch of autumn,
for survival.

vi.

Belly out on the frozen pond,
<u>frozen how long, how deep</u>,
watch for the shadow
of fish beneath
the surface—the possibility
of life, still, its glint,
any hint we're alive
and kicking.

But go, I'm right behind you,
right behind you waiting
for the New Year, the New
Testament, the fish caught
like a thoughtless word.
You <u>are</u> Jesus stepping
onto the water. I am
your apostle, my head
ablaze with learning.

The Gambler in Love /Robert Flanagan

says, Babe, I'm going to call you Dicey
and rattle your bones and mine
and make Mr. Bones in his black cutaway
hope for snake-eyes and wait his turn;

says, Dicey, I love it playing low-hole
when the derringer man leans forward
and the eyes I've watched watching each move
spot the ace of hearts, my hole card;

says, Babe, in this game there'll be no limit;
with Spring slipping on its green eye shade,
playing for the house and bumping my raise—
bluff or not, I'm sticking with it;

says, Dicey, you are my lucky double eagle,
flipped and spinning, I'll take you heads or tails.

A Prophet of Loss /Robert Flanagan

for Johnny Wink with his finer ear

I heard a voice I took to be God's
one time, lucky
to hear a damned thing over the stamp of machines
on our soot-bricked block where job
meant the swing-shift, a hounding foreman,
and pink slip fear.

My mutt greased by a mad cabbie,
my roof cracked, rain browning paper flowers,
my wife run off with some bush league pinch hitter,
I pitched my shovel at the coal pile—
"God Almighty!
I won't take life on these terms!"

And the sky stood still,
but for a girder swung home on a boom.
Okay, that voice said. Don't.

Circus/Robert Flanagan

We stand, mastiff-stolid, as they wrap
our wrists and hands in leather strapped
contrivances; pride, hate
and hard hours sparring are to keep us
shaking off jabs of pity or fear, guard up,
hot to wallop home lead-studded cestus.
Another slave, young cripple, opens a gate

and we blink into brassy glare, the bloody
circle of dirt, boxed-in,
two mounds of mud and stone done up as men
to face each other with something near
grins the gaping take as sneers
so caw approval: Here comes some action.
We are named enemies

(who in a more cordial country,
wisdom outstripping gaming war,
might knot cords of muscle over earth,
bear down a plow yoked oxen pull
and, evenings, cleansed, ungirdle
a melon-bellied, grape-nippled girl
and lay with her to father harmony

—we might even live
to stroll white-haired and oiled in delight
among the leathery-leaved green olives,
by Aphrodite granted life beyond the dead
legions croaking us on), so slog ahead,
square off in the stink of bears' guts,
chuck fists like hearts at the other's head.

Submarine Poem/Stuart Friebert

I

You think of moving the captured submarine
to a permanent berth alongside the museum
in your city. A retired engineer who spent
years on a plan to move the Eiffel Tower
volunteers a practical suggestion, so you
stop traffic on a lovely night in summer
and, as thousands watch, you inch the sub
across the outer drive. When it's in place
you introduce a famous naval commander
whose dedication address is piped ashore.

II

At first the interior of the sub
seems unbelievably complicated, a maze
of dials, valves and gauges, every
available foot of space occupied.
But listen to your guide, though you
lose a good deal of what she says and
she talks too much of how cramped
the quarters are, running her hand
over the checkered blue linen on the bunks,
and seems to idolize the enemy captain—
carefully she points to a picture of him
sitting on a horse on his farm in Bavaria—,
she will quit her job just before the tour
is over and press past you. Miss, stop!
Stop, Miss! everyone cries, plunged in grief.

III

The movies you see later in the museum theatre
are official navy films taken during the actual
battle. You press both hands on the slatted wooden
seat and stare up at the waves, they go higher and
your mind slides to the folding top on the washstand
which became the captain's desk when he lowered
the lid and drew the tiny blue curtain.

For Our Retarded Brothers/Stuart Friebert

Mom's dead, though they did get little Felix out
of her bag in time, a tumor on his spine, heaven
coming closer, the doctor asked to wash his hands.
The nurse powdered her nose and the rest of us ran
off, I made for the niche in the stairwell, wrote
lines on the window, could feel my nails growing,
my hair learning to stand on end. A storm brewed,
all the windows slammed. I yelled at Felix to turn
his TV off. He waddles out of his room, insisting
Adam and Eve were gardeners, insisting I take him
to the circus: he's heard we'll get in free if we
water the elephants. Past the horses taking long
strides on the outside, to the horses inside with
their tiny steps, I keep my eyes shut while Felix
pulls me along. From the worst seat in the house
we look down, the clown's pet sucking milk from
a bottle to the tune the seals play on their horns.

Felix started laughing then, the way he'd laugh when
we took him to the Japanese doctors (the pallor on
their faces when he laughed!). He kept on laughing,
nodding his small and formal head with an idea no one
else was ready for: In the end, he announced to half
the grandstand, Big cats usually do as they are trained.
But no one turned around to look at him, his face fell,
made it seemed from bread and cheese. Hardly stretching
arms, he hugged me like a man reaching through a manhole.
I hummed his verse for him.

        It isn't for us to say
        How people come to play,
        Dadah, dadee . . .

He pointed over at the lights that were going out all
around the tent top. Well, he said, They are very poor
people, I keep mine on all night. And pale, serious now,
he took my hand, edged us down between the rows of seats
across the sawdust to the center ring. I'm one of the
animals, he said, I'm one of the animals and I'm very thirsty.

Palm Sunday Tornado, 1964/Marilyn Gravett

1.

I wake in a sweat,
the smell of sausage downstairs.
I go with my brother
to watch the barometer drop.
He says everything is happening
too fast. Mother yells Church!
My dotted Swiss dress itches.
Outside even the newest daffodil wilts.
My brother shoves his fist out,
says, This is how it would feel in a cloud.
Mother comes looking for us,
says, My god, there's no air.
I don't question her.
I say I'm surrounded by moisture.
She asks me where my brother is.
I tell her he's in a tree
trying to climb into a cloud.

2.

Grandmother on the daybed
didn't sleep good. She says
even Mother's lace curtains
wouldn't move. Dad glares
at my brother in the kitchen, shoves
greasy meat patties to our plates.
We whisper across the table.
My brother says out loud,
There's going to be a tornado.
Grandmother groans. Mother cries
We're late! Dad says, Great,
now all the neighbors will want to sit
in our basement. I run my plate to the sink,
rinse it. The back of Dad's white shirt
is wet. My brother says,
You can always tell it's a tornado
when your own sweat won't dry up.

Running Things Backward/Marilyn Gravett

Here we go again: on the screen
my sister starts into a sit-spin,
finishes, begins to skate away,
her blades chipping forward

until my father in his projector's chair
literally giggles, and switches
the reels into reverse,
my sister's legs jerking backward

as if there were a magnet
in each clumsy heel tugging
at the back tips of her blades.
Here we go again: a sit-spin

from which she mysteriously lifts
and skates back-first off the frame.
What seemed so graceful and assured
in progression, in reverse

seems so pathetic and poignant,
a parody of a young figure skater.
My father only runs these movies forward
to be able to watch them back

and I suspect he, who turns seventy
this year, for all his glee,
is somewhere inside perfectly solemn,
running things backward

at the dizzying speed of a sit-spin.
Watching ourselves in reverse
is certainly humbling: here I go
on the screen, up and down

the same steps, looking silly
over my shoulder at my father, who follows
me in and out of the dark doorway
waving, and then is finally drawn back.

Menses/Marilyn Gravett

<u>for Emily</u>

There is a moon sliver tonight
in the hard sky, its silver wedge
come sudden and arresting
as your body with its new demands.

I look up, and my eye
can trace the whole
this sliver is a bright rim to,
then past the edges where the dark shoots off
to point itself around stars.

But when I look at you
I remember my own awkward self
at twelve telling my mother,
"I feel like a woman now,"

with the absolute certainty
I still feel
at the most uncertain times.
Who knows what pain you'll come to
understand your woman's self through.

But these stars, Emily, this slivered moon
with its timed pull to tides
inside you, are hard ties to a galaxy
of women all around you.

Lives of the Tribes/Terry Hermsen

1. Penobscot

Following these unscheduled
bursts of color and fruit
across summer,

coming full circle at last
to the thickets of rivers
coved at the edge of the ice and the sea.

2. Chippewa

Shadows in the reeds become familiar,
staying in one place
or two in the year. Wild

rice whacked clean over the cutting edge
of the canoe. Swollen ash from the winter fire
stains the late snow like a banner.

3. Creek

Hoes dipped in salt
water, bound with wet leather;
the central ceremonies of the corn.

Six-month summers
in which all healthy men and women
leave on the buffalo hunt.

4. Nachez

The old trick of the south
wind's pyramid (any floor means someone
must be below) moves in just,

cruel intent: the king's son must marry
a commoner, commoners may murder
their first born to ascend one rung.

5. Hopi

Six names of
corn for six floors
of the valley; each season's dance

returns one more ancestor. Like the sun into
the basket of night, wings of the dancer
fold into the earth-red kiva.

12 **Proverbs**/Terry Hermsen

1. When the tongue gets loose
   wisdom slides under the door.

2. Puppets dance behind us.

3. Swallow
   and the fish is yours

4. Deeds
   like weeds are our colonies
   And the revolution
   is long over

5. Count with thumbs
   and the day moves

6. Sitting on ice
   stirring the fire

7. Letters unanswered
   are mortar for a coffin

8. Fathers hold the kites

9. When the human is gone
    the rat comes in

10. All thoughts have a fuse

11. Memorize what moves
    and you carry
    distance

12. During the harvest
    go hungry

Call in the Night (a fable)/Terry Hermsen

Another name called me to this small hill,
where the moon has made a circle.
Not mine. Maybe the one that kept recurring
                            in the woods
and I'd hurry on, saying "he's gone,"
feeling vaguely guilty.

Now I am here, thinking whose mistake.

One more child needs a lullaby,
and the words gone again.

The night heat is thick in the well
and churns around my ladle like an ancient fish.

My mother was thirsty and sent me to this place
but the lost path has closed up like a wound.

I sit on a stump and drink
the gift I was supposed to bring back,

and the child who will not be comforted
becomes a small bird in my hand.

The Tunnel/Robert Hudzik

Silence is not a family trait; at least, not
In my family. I seem to be the only
Reticent, reserved member, poised on the edge
Of speech. Others often misinterpret
My reluctance as maturity. Perhaps, long ago,
Some ancestor witnessed an unspeakable act
& I am bound by blood to keep his dark secret.

When I was born, we lived in my mother's
Family home. Her brother was shipped to us
From halfway around the world with a fractured skull
To float in a sea of delirium
In the attic room above me. I did not cry,
I was a war baby, a new consciousness
Of peace & prosperity. My mother still smiles
How her first child learned to be quiet
Before he could speak.

        And when I think back on it,
My father was content, years later, to sit in his chair,
Smoking a cigar & reading the evening paper.
A snore would shake him from his dreams
& he'd become animate again
Outside his chosen element.

His father came to this country from Czechoslovakia,
A teenager with no English words in his head
To feel at home. Such a boy
Cannot speak his mind or make himself heard.
What is a son to make of his father's silence?
My father, like his father before him,
Learned to speak with his hands, at hard labor,
Thirty-six years of it, & to be honest
I don't understand how he stood it.

My father bent steel beams into arches
On a press that could slice a man in half.
The steel arches were used to support holes
Put through mountains by other men, other machines.
Years on the job curved his back & shoulders
Until they came to resemble the steel arches he made:
A human arch supporting a tunnel of silence,
Stretching from Czechoslovakia to the words on this page.

The Animals Within/Robert Hudzik

The undefined animals of our lives
Are gathering forces underground,
Each one donning the colors of surprise
For the time they rise within us

Into light: into the way the feet
Move in stride when the earth shifts,
Pumping, along the line of the leg
And up the spine to the heart,

Beating like a bird, in flight
To the brain, shooting off the top
Of the head like a star
Into a constellation of animals.

Self-Portrait With Glasses/Robert Hudzik

Of my four brothers, I am the only one
wearing glasses. In photographs without them,
I peer out through a pinched face as if trying
to place something I've forgotten, thinking hard
on my loss, while trying to keep something else
from leaking out, or sneaking in.

The world appears too large at times and I narrow
my line of vision by squinting: I see more clearly,
though only a part . . .
                              Years later, I will slip
my glasses on and stare back at the oval of light
for a moment; my eyes will not be able to hold such brightness
and will slide off to its edge,
where all shades gather into form and color,
to where I live.

Until I Met You/James C. Kilgore

Until I met you
I wanted to watch Hawaiian women
    dancing to sea wind and ukelele music;
I wanted to see sensuous red California suns
    bow in silky splendor
    before pastel pacific characters.
I wanted to dance to Nigerian drums,
To feast on the luscious grapes of France,
To drink coconut wine in Ghana,
To pray in the temples of Jerusalem:
I dreamed of the glories of exotic and holy
    places,
Until I met you.

No Ordinary Beginning/James C. Kilgore

I sit
    alone
    with poetry
(She seems, like God, always near)
    and thoughts of you
(Lying among chrysanthemums, spider
    plants, cacti, and begonias with blue or
    brown or black or purple passions).
As we watch maples dance in the snow,
Poetry snuggles close and whispers
That some night or day you may need healing
    hands:
If you do,
Know this:
I make house, apartment, or condominium
    calls;
And I shall bring you strong hands and
    Christmas cacti or red cyclamen
And we shall begin—

We shall begin—
It will be no ordinary beginning.

An Awkward Silence/James C. Kilgore

The woods were gone from the land;
They had torn down the house
Where I was born.
Bushes stood stubborn
    on the level land of my adolescent years.
Standing with my son
    at the edge of that early life,
I rebuilt the house,
Created the noise of love,
Planted the silent beauty
    of a vegetable garden,
Lit the kerosene lamp in the room of my
    dark past.

My son seemed a bit annoyed
    at my rebuilding, on bush-covered land,
    a verbal picture of the past;
    So I ended the story,
    Told him why we left the place
    to go "Up North."

Driving past the dead sawmill
    where my father had earned our bread,
I felt an awkward silence
    riding between me and my city-born son.

So I ended the story,
Told him why we left the place

The Real Ideal/Joel Lipman

Eh, you want to buy a sweating negro?
Come around back past the Chinese tea roses
& I'll show you some hot arms and legs,
one with a belly wet as the ocean.

Eh, you want a cupboard vast as God's brow,
fragrances from the spice shoppe,
air foul as a drunkard's morning fart?
I can put on a platter fit for a Bar Mitzvah!

You like to dance allegro or presto,
stroll to the del-Vikings, pedro?
I got a palamino out back & a Chevy 409
in the carport. Varoom, my hands are clean as talcum.

If I sound like a skinflint merchant,
crusty as an armadillo without the kiss of a poet,
you're right. But look, jack,
you want tomato-flavored aspirin, I got 'em,

you want vapors from the Pope's mass, I got that.
Some folks pride themselves on piety
& others hoe purple gardens of eggplant.
Me, I'd hustle mama's bridgework for a buck,

then sell her back the breeze she sucks.
Eh, you want Coca Cola from Albania.
or lettuce dusted with Modesto radium?
In this land anything goes—you get what you get.

translitic from Julian del Casal "Idilio realista"

THAT, PERHAPS
IT, WAS DIFFER-
ENT, AS IF A
NOVEL OE JOY
WAS TODAY'S
PAPER OR WERE OX-
IDE SLOWLY
TURNING
AN UN-
EASY &
LOVELY
BLUE
HAR-
BOR
THE DOGS
GRINDING SNARL
WHERE MUN-
ITIONS MER-
CHANTS
SLEEP NUDE.
AND SECURITY, YOU
ASK ABOUT
THAT? POETRY.
LIKE A CANNON
UNDER MY
TONGUE &
A 45 IN THE
COFFEE CAN.
HEROES?—THE
RUDEST SON-OE-
A-BITCH IN
TOWN, SO
LONG AS
HE'S
PURE OF
HEART &
NOT TOO STU-
PID. I'M HORRIFIED
BY NOTHING BUT
BUT DOING
NOTHING IN THE
MIDST OF
HORROR.
MORNINGS, I
SPORTS
WORK FORCE

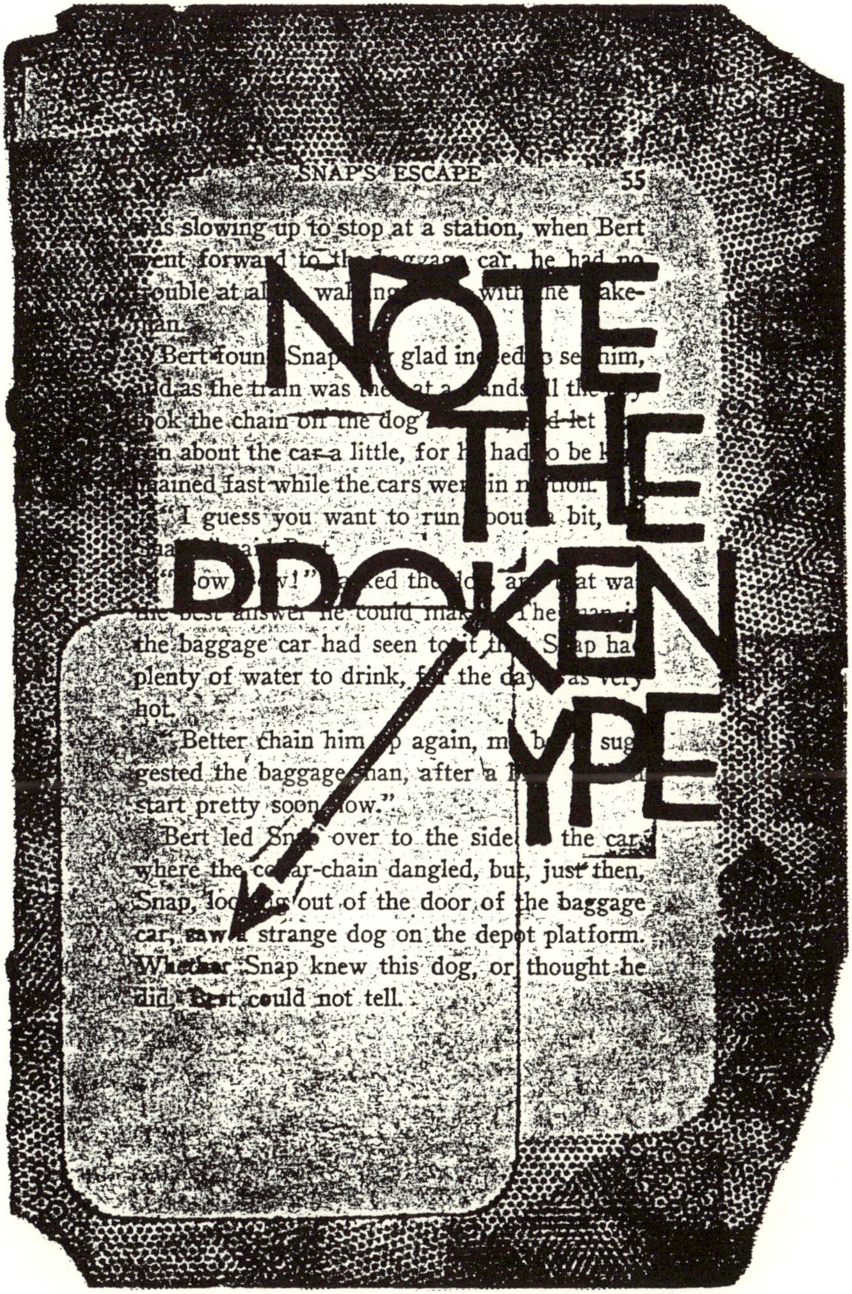

SNAP'S ESCAPE   55

...as slowing up to stop at a station, when Bert
went forward to the baggage car, he had no
trouble at all... walking... with the brake-
man.
   Bert found Snap... glad indeed to see him,
and as the train was then at a standstill the...
took the chain off the dog... and let
...run about the car a little, for he had to be kept
chained fast while the cars were in motion.
   "I guess you want to run about a bit,
Snap, said Bert.
   "Bow wow!" barked the dog, and that was
the best answer he could make. The man in
the baggage car had seen to it that Snap had
plenty of water to drink, for the day was very
hot.
   "Better chain him up again, maybe," sug-
gested the baggage man, after a bit, "we'll
start pretty soon now."
   Bert led Snap over to the side of the car,
where the collar-chain dangled, but, just then,
Snap, looking out of the door of the baggage
car, saw a strange dog on the depot platform.
Whether Snap knew this dog, or thought he
did, Bert could not tell.

NOTE THE BROKEN TYPE

Sir Walter Raleigh Goes to The Movies/Joel Lipman

The line outside the movies is slower
than justice in the central square of this town.
And from the way everybody talks,
chirping and vibrating like tropical fruits,
raucus jungle fifty yards past the restaurant,
why, you'd think they'd smoked the day's last cigar
ten or twenty times since breakfast.
Half-notes from the waiters calling their orders,
half-notes from attendants handling the cars,
half-notes from the theater interior
where I sense there is swordplay.

          Just yesterday,
a fat diplomat took me to see the Fifth Dimension,
"a peach of a combo to throw pies at,"
he called the performance. Myself, I thought
a gas, better than the dancing dolls
that man is selling off the sidewalk under the marquee.
Better than those crummy tacos and sluts
they call opera singers. Divinas!, my touchas.

          This place is magnificent,
so dark a child could turn into fungus. A felon
about to drop off the gallows should have a chance
to see a technicolor movie like "The Gold Of El Dorado."
Then he could die.

And the sound system
beats fornicating with beasts. Clearly there is liberation
in all these masturbating fists.
Viva libertad! Viva libertad! Yet,
how to describe the screen—a vast possibility
of sugary canvas, an enormous space filled with camps,
the middle of America, horses, sky and expanse.
If I were not so fat I would run down the aisle
and touch it, leap through the flickering
light like a homespun gymnast agoof
under those heavenly stars in the ceiling.

Closing credits, how discouraging.
I feel simpleminded standing in line again—
if I were a kid, it'd all be different.

translitic from Heberto Padilla "Los ultimos recuerdos
de Sir Walter Raleigh en la Torre de Londres"

Old Habits/Howard McCord

January thaw and a starling
emerged from a snowbank stiff and black.
Dogs found him and played tag
all morning, excited by the feathers
in their mouths and the smell life
leaves when it dies.

The dogs will eat plastic buckets, beer
cans, sticks, and tatters of rugs.
They're only six months old.
But as we all do, they like
best something live, or
once alive. Same principle keeps us
gnawing at love or religion
no matter the juice is gone,
it doesn't move and tastes
like a wet board.

Directions/Howard McCord

You can begin by turning
a corner and running into
a man imitating the moon,
or leading a fox
on a long blue string.

There are books which
tell you how to accomplish
the permissible, and
others that warn you
not to.

The man imitating
the moon, for instance,
was never seen
again.

Off a Bit/Howard McCord

The beat caught
like a bird in a mangle
my heart goes green
under the tourniquet
of losing my way.

A cat in a burlap
bag can't enjoy the view
of a river, nor
a bank clerk gagging
on a 12-gauge
the humor of an unsecured
loan.

Perhaps the pig
strung by the grind-
stone's sparks
remembers his
breakfast, but
a man who is losing
his way
can remember nothing
important at all.

Light at the Beginning of the Tunnel
/Robert McGovern

"At the annual awards assembly at
Black River . . . , valedictorian Barbara
Betleski . . . said she felt that she had not
been accepted by her classmates and that
she was never considered as part of the
class.
"In the short . . . speech, Miss Betleski
said that she would hold 'only sad
memories' of her four years at the school
and her graduating class of 1974. She
turned down $600 worth of scholarships
for being valedictorian and having the
best senior grade average."
Ashland Times-Gazette

Barbara, struggling from your name,
You took for truth
A world where knowledge and love
Hold fast to receding time
And now is the object of then.

But you grew in a pastless age
Where pratfall serves for wit
And one's own thing, T-grouped to same,
Subserves the dimming mind;
Where education panders sloth
That violates Minerva's creed
And Eros' holy hope,
Cassandra rasping as usual;
And where to pot be Pepsi young
Is owning life.

We poets, wording to realize
Our teeming brains,
Are aware of what you've learned—
That little heed is paid,
No praise, to the sullen craft.

You got it well by rote in school
And came to poem your saddened wit
As prologue to a darkening age.

We welcome you,
Another point of ironic light
To sustain us as we swim
The black river of the world.

Ice on the Pond/William McLaughlin

She had been immersed since that spring
her blushes were dropped as defenses.
Reeds at the edges demanded a count of
clustered snails, changeable data levels

she carried into the central deep
as reports to the eyeless proteuses
slick in their bottom muck. She measured
each strand of frogs eggs, soon

tabulated tadpoles, lost consciousness
of the sheltering water, that support for
her totaling rounds. If it warmed by day
she rose to bask on a bland surface

glinting needles, to sink in the
cooling currents of night away from
a vapid glance of moon. She stroked
a clean stroke there, pressure

shaping the contents of her skin,
saw without recognition a slight
crustiness veiling at the rim of
things. She gave the disruptive eyeless

in depth her full attention, though
above her hair-draped body the sealing
thickened. When the circuitry of regime
at last sent her looking for openings,

nose pressed into the air space of a scant
scream, mind (that had masked performance)
asked one question in the end, asked
what now is the intention of water.

Sittings/William McLaughlin

Red ribbons tied
in the town park
remind of nineteen
rapes under its trees.

Yellow ribbons
fly on posts
by the river of
twelve bodies floating.

Black ribbons circle
the fenced closure
of our power plant
split at the seams.

Purple waves over
eighty-nine road
intersections; green
where the maples stood.

Orange is for
what's kinky; blue
the stolen away;
pink is our catch-all.

Like bright pennants
that flash and flare,
a soft breeze
flickers the messages.

Until the cold gray
changing wind of
normal acceptance
shows we're on fire.

Dornava Palace/William McLaughlin

(Yugoslavia)

Its principal chambers open through
the art of illusionism—doors, gods,
wings, vistas of worlds not there;
but the grandest murals in Slovenia
have no tourist trade.

Parents arrive. A short wait
in the vestibule brings out
one's own autistic child,
mongoloid, or pinhead. Otherwise,
the State allows no visitors.

For an hour the family walks
by sun-bright cornfields,
or by the palace walls, the arbors,
under gateway arches of fat
clambering cherubs dripping grapes.

Father labors to see affection in
the crooked smile, drives them
for holiday down a lined avenue of
trees, straight trees, more than
lingering years no mother counts.

After calling hours, who can guess
which buckled limb and skewered eye
picks 2-D chrysanthemums,
opens the tricked-up doors,
and tries those wings.

Four Patients/William McMillen

"St. Elmo"

<u>Crazy Elmo</u>
    nurses
      whispered
          confiscating

camels, four roses, Ohio kitchen matches

         still

one Saturday morning
he burned his room
Up

    <u>Crazy Elmo</u>
         They shouted
           spit
           splash
           safe

The room was a total

         loss
         but

Elmo
stood off to the side
smoking like a chimney
smelling like a rose

         whistling
         like
         crazy

"Carolyn"

She wept to death
of a sadness no one
could diagnose dreaming
of an island where it
rained too many days
and all the nights
until her whole body
wept the same song,
the same rain, months
in a hospital bed
too dry to stay alive
drowning in her own dreams.

"Robin's Egg"

                                 Fried

            scrambled

    hard-boiled

    Robin's brain had a friend inside
    who refused to leave the nest

    The cat scanned the scene   but
    no   hope, robin egg blue eyes

    Still . . . breakfast never tasted as sweet
    and the birds' songs inside were

    clear
                        light
                                    Endless

"Michael"

Ruptured disc.
The surgeon said it was like a jelly donut
without its jelly. Michael was insulted.
Metaphors were <u>his</u> province—
    the tools of a poet.
    Would he ever try and compose
    a poem with a scalpel?
    No.
Save the scalpel for his tender back;
save the metaphors for his ruptured poems.
    Disc is too bad:
    a donut without its jelly;
    a surgeon without his scalpel;
    a poet without his back.
Rupture ruptured. Michael turned over
stepped on a crack and broke his line
and wrote again and again and again.

An Old Sportswriter Celebrates His Fiftieth Anniversary of Covering the Yale-Dartmouth Game
/Jack Matthews

One thousand and one hundred starting lineups
of boys run out onto some field that is as
green as it ever was and windy and the crowd
as drunk and happy and irreverent and the
bulldog has been fed right before the game
exactly thirty-one times so that it will
squat and dolefully defecate between the
ten and forty yard line by the running track
that surrounds the gridiron like a moat
and all those styles of uniform and youth
mingled in a huddle of time telescoped
remembered on this anniversary date by an
old man who's afflicted by angina and
a certain bewilderment here in front of his
typewriter commissioned to retell that old story
still once again of old Eli and the Indian
and how it is always new and of the stuff of myth
and still undecided even after the awful hour
is past and already boys in locker rooms
are waiting to crowd those sweating fathers
out forever while the band plays and pennants flap.

The Instant/Jack Matthews

you kiss her, her face disappears.
And later, at the heart of all that breathing,
you are both anonymous, collating lust,
while the earth turns dark beyond the corona
of your heat, and your privacy glows.
From a great distance, the two of you tangled
in that damp agony, your limbs spread out,
look like a child's large drawing of a star—
smoldering, shuddering light, six-pointed.

That Poems Should be Printed On Recyclable Paper is Only Right/Jack Matthews

Consider the alternatives of yesterday's truth
still staring at us like a sunburned eye that
can't blink. Or, how about abandoned passions
burying their noses like dogs in the old discarded
clothing of pensioners long dead?

Think of the pleasure you might get in crumpling
this poem up, right now, and tossing it like some
dittoed notice into the commodious tolerance of trash.

Everything is biodegradable if you wait long enough;
but I'm talking about the joys of evanescence—
the word flipped away like a caught spy's cigarette;
I'm talking about messages going back into the
elemental mix, allowing their fumes and raptures
to live alone, breathed forth like ancient souls
to wander down the streets and alleys of every future
city that all your unborn sons and daughters could
ever believe in when they step outside at morning.

Dawn—After the Argument/Julie L. Miller

Quiet the flicker of hands in dismay.
Sleepless on my side of the bed, I lie
and watch the thin thread of gold slip into day.

Last night no sun set; the sky growled with gray
clouds. He made angry love with sharp, quick sighs.
Quiet—the flicker of hands in dismay.

Now all the sun's fury is caught in one ray,
his hip outlined by the goldening sky.
Watch the thin thread of gold slip into day.

He's still clenched with anger. I want to play
my fingers down the keys of his bare spine,
but quiet the flicker of hands in dismay.

My mouth is dry; he's pushed the sheets away,
it's so hot. Some mornings I wonder: why
watch the thin thread of gold slip into day?

Before the alarm whines I dress, but stay
to fix his coffee. It is how I
quiet the flicker of hands in dismay,
watch the thin thread of gold slip into day.

What the Visiting Poet Said/Julie L. Miller

Disregard everything
Anyone's ever told you.
Shift this comma two words
To the right. Watch your weak
Line breaks. Get rid of the saccharine
Which means any mention
Of Grandma Miller and the farm.
Delete. Delete. Remember,
Sound and sense, nothing
Is arbitrary, but scratch
<u>Something</u> in the second line.
You have no natural rhythm;
Try clapping to count the syl-lab-les.
Don't capitalize each line.
Don't write about sex,
God, or your dog dying.
Now you are ready to relax
and let the lines flow.

It Happens in Slow Motion/Julie L. Miller

When her hip pops out of socket
the pain surprises her. Bone on bone
is sharp and gritty; she pictures a knife
against a whetstone. The tendons
in her neck strain against her skin
like finely twisted twine as she screams
into the gag. She tries to kick
into the air, into the socket,
but his knee grinds into her thigh,
bone against bone against cement.
Her eyes, too dry to close,
stare as he poises above her.
The silver chain he wears dangles
between her breasts. Finally,
on his first thrust, the leg twists free
and the bone slides into joint.

Sunset XII/Nick Muska

<u>for William Kloefkorn in Nebraska</u>

Drinking flat champagne—Californian Brut
Stoned on the best sensemillia, lemons & Bougainvillea,
the scent of drunk lovers in the dark night air
Key West, February
Let George Washington cross <u>his</u> icey rivers
This Caribbean be the cross I'll bear.
Tell me of "American grit"
I'll tell you of rawboned sunburnt citizens
tattooed women nude under thin cotton,
island crazies, conga drummers named Pedro,
reciting shrimper poets armed with beer
palmettoed among the delicate, hungry,
exotic flora of the glitzy night.
Hemingway, Crane, Stevens, Tenn. Williams
all came south, some never returned.
Hell, Kerouac, too, descended to Florida
—every good Canuck's dream—
Found his final fountain here.

We all got our ways to the spring, Bill
You find yours
I'll find mine.

XIII <u>The Cherelles</u> Live at <u>The Monster</u>
/Nick Muska

<u>St. Valentine's Day</u>

Tangled with the gay crowd
on the tacky disco floor

broke my heart
"Baby, It's You"

Shala
lala lala lala
la la la

"This is Dedicated to the One I Love"

(swoon)

"Soldier Boy"
in pink satin pea caps

Heartmasks & roses
Danish honey-butter pitchblende lips
glitter & toreador pants
24 years on the road
a million one night stands
a billion singles

I'll be true to you.

David Allen Coe Gives Key West
a Free Street Concert/Nick Muska

Sun flames out off Mallory Pier.
Duval jammed with black t-shirt riders,
Mammas, marijuana,
Megasound thumping over
Paleblue airbrushed cactus&prairie custom Greyhound.

David Allan shakes his locks,
Strums in strutstance like an Assyrian bowman
in an electric limelit Dallas suit,
Growls out raspy sugar wounds.
Sad, sadder, saddest
easy swingin' country tunes—
Bikers go wild with grief.

Big tit t-shirt legend in the down-from-Daytona crowd:
"Biker's Old Ladies Give Better Head."
Now 16 year old Dori from Big Pine Key
glows like a radium virgin
in white lit ole opry gown,
Whines blue light from her ivory country fiddle.

Sunset totalled out, the afterstreet
crackles with cans, plastic cups,
paddy wagons stuffed with drunks.
Pale the steel Harleys
Pale the ladies of the chromium horsemen.

February 21, 1982
Key West

Reverie/Jane Piirto Navarre

Living, it's hard to find
get meaning from it living
it it's hard to figure out
the meaning there must be
meaning, right? else why all
the churches else all this
living has no meaning
we say describe experience

we can't read philosophy
anymore: the jargon tiny
machinations of innumerable
egos. we watch tv see movies
avoid potholes on roads try
to get from one place to another
the museum read journals
talk talk try to place
to see what belief means

we read science fiction novels
in the kitchen discuss megatons
massacres sport bull
market barrows and gilts
living, it's hard to find
get meaning from the stands
we take mushy
as spring ground in the woods
we wear boots don't mind
living it, it's hard to
else why all the churches?

Runners/Jane Piirto Navarre

all the lovely young jocks
at the universe

-ity's indoor track
in their long strides

passing me up
their tibia fibula femur

their bare naked backs
tight little gluteus

maximus dimpled
trapezei, their hamstrings

their hidden diaphragms
that probably pant

To a Sleeping Child/Jane Piirto Navarre

you sleep.
2 a.m., the mid of night
I must flash this light
to see that your pupils
are each the same size

your swollen face
bashed into blacktop alley
your inner lips flared
with stitched tooth gashes
your scabbing cheeks

smashed nose and knees
foetal you lie
pillow covered
with a bloody towel
you cannot suck your thumb tonight

your friend brought your bike home
a neighbor carried you
home crying "mama"
mama mama mama mama
I almost cried for my own

at the sight of you
you and your trust
your arms thrust at me
believing I'd make it all
all right

as mothers are reputed to do
who else does a child have?
who does anyone have, ever?
mamamama
we own each other

irrevocably parent and child
unbinding unwinding
I know this
and am not eased
knowing it

Story/Gary Pacernick

This gray haired woman with blue numbers on her arm
Gives the boy with watery blue eyes a bagel.
When he puts a quarter in her hand, she starts to cry.
That old man, wrapped in the zebra striped shawl,
Only his black eyes and beard showing, shakes his finger
At the boy who stands next to him, flapping his wings.
There are holes in the old man's shoes.
His toes are crying children.
Suddenly all the children fly away.
A vulture hovers over the synagogue.

Babel/Gary Pacernick

Isaac Babel is riding with bloodthirsty Bolshevik soldiers.
The settings are poetic: sun, moon, stars
Shining like sabbath candles, frogs croaking
Like old peddlers, wheat flapping in the breeze.
But Babel records, too, the severed head of the old Jew
And the hurt, half-dead cry of his daughter:
"And where in the world is there a better father?"
"Come on Babel, get your ass in the saddle
Or your head will roll on top of that old kike's head."
Babel is off and riding, telling funny stories
To his fellow revolutionary soldiers,
Stalin glaring from that rising sickle moon.

The Air Force Museum/Gary Pacernick

Three hundred Baptist Sunday school children
Are hanging from the wings of the giant B-36
A line of families waits to enter
"The world's most decorated bomber:
1,500,000 tons of bombs on target."
It's a mausoleum of bombshells,
Meters, dials, belts, tin seats.
A man stops to aim a turret gun.
Back outside, a tiny observation plane
Hovers in mid-air from the ceiling.
"The Strawberry Bitch" is tattooed to the ribs of a fighter bomber.
There are pictures of the Glenn Miller Band
And mementos of World War II prisoners of war:
A cardboard pendulum clock, a soldier's painting of the blue Venus,
Notes pencilled on the back of cigarette wrappers, a poem.
The movie of the day shows an Eighth Air Force bomber crew
Dodging black flak over Germany for the twenty fifth time,
Dropping bombs on the enemy's factories and bridges.
This is the dark Disneyland of war waiting to be reborn.

Sandbox Burial/Gary Pacernick

One by one the children in the sandbox bury themselves
And the queer obtrusive man whom the grownups distrust
Who haunts the park and knows every child's name
Puts a dead branch on every mound of sand

The Last House in Luna Pier/Frank Polite

"On this Yao sent away Huan Tau
to Ch'ung hill, the Chiefs of the
Three Miao to San Wei, and banished
the Minister of Works to the Dark
Capital, so unequal had they been
to cope with the world."
       Chaung Tzu

1/

From the last house in Luna Pier
Clear to the moon
I am alone.

Stuffed with sorrow, the couch
Rolls over in the weeds
Like a huge dog.

An owl barks
Up the wrong tree, woo woo . . .

Gathering, gathering, the sea
Unravels my life,
Why are you here?
             The moon
Touches my lips with its
Spoon of salt

       And I cannot answer.

2/

Old woman picking through my trash.
A grey November lace cast over
Her rags, and a hat like a clamshell.

Leaning on the screendoor, I ask
What are you looking for?

Whatever is left, she says,
Treasure, redeemables. Shaking her head,
You've thrown away good clothes,
Half-eaten apples; here's a loaf
Of bread barely out of its wrapper.

I wonder who she is,
Pearl and moonstone rings on her
Fingers, gathering, gathering . . .

3/

Friends come to visit,
Evening of wine, hashish, music.

Law can be poetry.
Poetry cannot be law.
Law cannot judge poetry.
Poetry judges law.

What we talk about is forgotten.

The hermit star hangs
Its lantern above the waters.
The lighthouse turns

On a pile of rocks in the harbor.

4/

Unlike rivers and streams
The sea does not take sides.
It is not for human beings
To bridge for an hour's
Convenience,

Nor does it spin at the end
Of a line to nurture Egypt.
Hung on a wall, the sea
Will tell the fairest of all,
Nothing . . .

About Art or Science
Or simply where you are,
Nothing. To cross,

You must take direction
From a star, light years off,
Or be lost.

Perfect, Anonymous, Divine,
The sea reflects
At great depth,
Itself.

And when it thinks, phantoms
Pour into our dreams.
And when it speaks, listen:
Selfish Selfish Selfish

5/

The pen will now sail off
By itself, where love has gone.
My fingers return to my hand
Where they were born.

This is my last poem, I know it.

I grip the dark edge
Of a skillet. Ancestors, ancient,
Call me down to burnt iron, yes.
They whisper, <u>hard times.</u>
They scatter bones to show me

The way it will be from now on.

With a twist of my wrist
A domestic fire flares up. Gas is
Quick to ignite, and reliable.
A meter in the cellar ticks,
Measuring my use.

This is it, at last, I'm home.
The eggs I crack
Will back up against my heart
Like unborn poems.

6/

I reveal myself through a shared vision.
Now it is myself again, alone,
The vision shut down like a night
In a drunk tank.

It is lonelier than I know.

I lean closer to the earth. I go
One step at a time.

A night like this, I cherish my soul, my
Quietness. I listen to myself
Listening to myself,

And the loneliest I know is this:

The moon is a mailed fist,
The wind cold. I am delivered
Like a sand dune to another part
Of the desert.

7 / Lantern

Next year I'm forty years old.
I don't know what hump I'm over.
<u>To have made it this far,</u> what
Does that mean? Where am I?

Where have I been? Like you,
I've been places, New York, Asia,
Great fields uncut by wire
Or river, mountains leaping up,

And O yes, oceans. I felt my way
Deeply into each, into the mind
Shafts permitted me, into
A flower (perfect on mescaline,

I laughed & wept for hours),
Into the tenderness of people . . .
I've loved, worshipped stones,
Written poems to moon and stars,

And depending on the deep and dark
Of my downheartedness, I lit
A flame in my forehead like a toad,
Imagining myself, at various

Times, Lord of Earth, Light in
The Forest, even . . . God.
Down the road with my lantern, I
Lifted up the broken, the poor,

The ignorant, the hopeless, only
To come down to this: to be all of
Them myself, at once. So what's
It all about? I don't ask anymore . . .

I am one with the insect and cloud.
I beg my life to lay me down at last,
Gently if possible, or fast, the way
A horse, plunging into darkness,

Kicks a stone out of its path.

8 / Luna Pier

A sea change leans against the pier
In tumult. <u>I know why I'm here</u>.
Cold streams, contending with the warm,
Grip the rocks as never before
In my life, and hurl up salt at my door.
What drifts in now is mine, cut loose,
Thrown overboard, or drowned;
A wooden spar, a bleached bone, a yard
Of torn sail like an indecipherable
Parchment. Even a shoe drifts in, kicked
Around out there God knows how long.
I listen now. I witness. I do not
Touch or twist at the integrity of each
Survival. It is enough to have arrived
At all, embodying sea changes;
To stagger ashore, free, cured of use;
Simply to be, <u>itself</u>, a green bottle,
A message delivered, a sailor, like me.

9/

I promise a poem to a blue heron.

Every morning, for a week or so, it stood
In the marsh grasses outside
My window, perfectly
Still,

One leg poised in the air
As if it were about to kneel, or dip
Its quill into a blue pool,
Or disappear . . .

I never saw it move.

And when I turned elsewhere, to poems,
Or coffee, or pacing the room,
The heron would be gone.

That last morning . . .
Solitude of the blue heron.
Black branches of trees,
A light snow falling

Through eaves of Heaven.

10/

My face inside
my cupped hands.
My fingertips
at my hairline
like soft pods
tapping the earth.
What is alive
at such times?
The night, the
silence of thought
wrapped in itself.
My skull is
a shell tuned
to emptiness, like
Love itself
before desire
created all things.

The Green Tree/James Reiss

Ever since my daughters started to walk
I have had increasing difficulty with my eyes.
I remember the day Wendy took her first steps, when
she said "bamboo" and waddled over to pat the rusty bumper

of a truck, I could barely make out the writing
scrawled in dirt on the trailer and had trouble focusing
as she stepped into its shadow.
The morning in Maine when she raced down the beach

and splashed into the ocean before I could reach her,
I actually mistook her for another little girl in pink
whom—I am sorry to say—I began leading slowly out of the water.
Then there is Jill: when she first walked I remember

looking at her and thinking, "I am a camera fading back, back."
Years later when she would go rollerskating with Wendy
my eyes were so bad I could no longer tell
where the sidewalks left off and my daughters began.

By now everything has faded into fine print. I
have been to a doctor who says he is also troubled,
but has sons. My only son died three days after
birth, weighing two pounds. His name was

Jeffrey, but I have always preferred to call him "Under-the-Earth"
or, especially on rainy days, "Under-the-Sod." In fact,
sometimes I catch myself repeating these words: "My only son,
Under-the-Sod, is playing over there by the green tree."

A Candystore in Washington Heights/James Reiss

One of those two-bit luncheonettes on a nothing
block with Coca-Cola
signs and an owner who looks like Groucho Marx.
One of those holes in the heat
wall of summer
up the hill from the Bridge and its lighthouse.
One of those pre-War leftovers
that specialize in Hamilton Beach malted mixers
and fans on the ceiling
where BLTs were always
a quarter and the owner, Levine, still stoops
with a cigar that has been rotting
in his hand for thirty years.

    Levine of the gray suspenders,
    Levine of the white shirt in summer that is always fading,
    Levine of the brown teeth and baldspot, scooping ice cream
          from your old horse of a freezer:

By the magazine rack,
by the blackening collection of comics
and dustmice, a boy who has paid for his malted
with his palms up, letting
you dip for dimes,
has his nose in Wonder Woman.
Today he will sneak it under his T-shirt.
While you are screwing the ketchup
or cursing the Germans,
he will slink out the door
                   with the turn
of your cheek.

Locked in his bedroom
for hours, he will pore over Wonder
Woman in Jersey City, Batman
Trapped in the Cave of Lost Guano—
and will rise to his mother's
shouts for dinner only when the scraps
of paper on his desk tell everything
he knows about bridges in sunlight.

    Levine of the frankfurter fingers,
    Levine of the dishrag and dills,
    Levine of the Life-Savers, Charms, the small cherry Cokes
        that are never enough:

In one of those dustbins
swept up from the gutters of streets
not far from the river of summer,
I stole the cigar from your mouth
and the hundred wads of Chiclets
stuck under your counter.
I stuffed them under my T-shirt.
I kneaded them in my pocket.
I shaped them into a bridge.
I sat at my desk as I shaped
the sun-silver towers, the roadway,
the lighthouse as red as a matchtip—
for you, Levine, for you.

from "Making Scenes"/Michael J. Rosen

<u>November</u>

Now, without snow, the trees seem bare:
there are no leaves but the wind is
warm through the window and sluggish
as bees that catch inside your hair.

Something you said perseverates
on the pages though I turn them,
though I look away, staring out
as if on rain or air about

to rain. I phrase what I should say
and then forget it. Already
the room is too dark for reading.
Besides, something might be settled

by someone giving in, turning
on a light. Someone does. Between
us the space shows up like a fault
neither overlooks or admits:

it keeps there in the middle.
What can be decided now or
in the morning for all the leaves
we might expect the trees to bear?

from "Making Scenes"/Michael J. Rosen

<u>December, the Botanical Gardens</u>

What blossoms now blossoms only in name:
the garden is all perennial signs
and branches pruned back to the barest limbs,
survival being patience or what's innate.
<u>Tea, cabbage, chinese</u>, each rose we picture
blooms red or pinkish buds or rosy pinked ones
above the same brown wintering leaves, still pinioned
and now so scarce, we'd think them worth protection
if they were lovely. There's little else to see:
some mallards stored beneath a miniature footbridge,
an emerald hot house nurturing all the privileged—
we're cold, we're missing more than something green.
What blossomed will blossom again, an instinct
left in the early Kingdoms: the child's, the Plant.

Solo I Will Stand in Winds that Choose to Take Me
/Joel Rudinger

Solo I will stand in the winds that choose to take me.
Stand me in the winds. Will I solo in the winds that take.
Stand in the winds, solo I will choose to solo.
Solo in the winds that choose to take me I will stand.

Stand, I will solo in the solo winds to choose.
Take me, solo; solo will I stand in the winds that choose;
Choose to take me, winds, that solo I will stand.
I will stand in the winds that solo choose to take me.

Take me, solo, choose. Solo will the winds to choose.
Take me, I will stand in the solo winds that choose to solo.
Winds to take and solo will I take to stand.
Winds, winds, in solo stand I take to me that choose to will.

Solo in the will, choose to stand the winds that take.
Solo I will solo in the winds to solo in the solo winds.
Winds, winds' will, I stand to take me solo.
Take me, take me, stand I wind, choose me solo, solo winds.

I will choose the winds' solo, solo choose the will.
Choose to take me, in the winds that will me solo.
That stand I take, the solo winds that choose to will me,
To choose me, to stand in the will, stand in the solo will.

Sitting for Margaret/Joel Rudinger

"No, no," she says. "Don't move. It's hard
enough to draw someone under sixty."
So I sit, quietly aware that shadows creep toward me
as her pencil whispers over the rough paper.

"How do you see me?" I ask without words.
The pencil growls and scratches deep into the fiber.
"You never know," she says, "how it will turn out."

"Old men are easiest to draw." She glances up.
"All their years of work and loss, pain and loving
trench their faces with lines of a lost beauty.
It stands out like rows of wheat unharvested
withered from too much richness.
And, Joel, I have looked often into old men's eyes;
those deep wrinkles drawn down by gravity and time
frame not eyes, no eyes, but an immortal soul."

Suddenly her fingers jam; the pencil's lead snaps off.
"No, no," she says. "The lip. The eyes. And—here, look—
something else about the mouth."
"No smile," I say. "That's not what I meant at all."
"It's so hard to do someone under sixty," she says again.
"Experience has not yet undone the sinews. Your face
has not yet unfolded to your grace."

It's five o'clock. She packs away her pencils, gum, and pad.
"We'll try again tomorrow." Then she goes.
Gone, I wonder blankly where the smile was I thought I had.
And she knows.

Boardwalk/Elizabeth Spires

Tonight
these messages
we pencil into picture postcards
to send to friends
who live inland, who never visit the ocean,
seem scrawls of omission: <u>dolphins sighted</u>
<u>and lost . . . fishermen on the jetty in yellow raincoats . . .</u>
<u>the boardwalk's arcade of lights . . .</u>
We sleep in a rented house
that offers no protection against nightmare:
the black wave high as a house
rising against us, or fog
walling us in
until, like sleepwalkers,
we break the windows with our hands,
and let the night rush in to fill each room's emptiness.

<u>An arcade of lights . . .</u>

We can go to the shooting gallery,
a Wild West Saloon, and aim for the piano player
frozen over an upright
riddled with bullet holes. Hit the spittoon,
and his head spins round,
his left foot taps out time
to a fragment of honky-tonk played over and over.
We can ask Sister Lisa to advise, impersonating
lives we've studied on the boardwalk,
gestures of boredom and desire.
She'll open our hands like old maps,
look into our palms and lie, pretending
we'll have many children.
We can have our picture taken by a photographer
with a trunkful of costumes. He'll pose us,
stone-sober, in front of painted backdrops
from plays and novels: a cherry orchard,
a train station, a <u>fin de siecle</u> drawing room.
His old-fashioned flash
blinding us, so that we stagger
back onto the boardwalk holding each other,
unsure which way to go.
On either side of us, more mirrors
and lights, more hours to kill
until the boardwalk closes at one or two.

Tomorrow
we'll sleep till noon. Or maybe
I'll wake early and quietly leave you
to walk the empty boardwalk, arms around myself,
reassured by the clarity of morning,
gulls scavenging, the smell of coffee
coming from the coffeeshop.
I'll mail the stack of postcards
left on the nightstand, dating them
Yesterday, Today, or Tomorrow,
pencil two stick figures into your favorite view—
a curving panorama of the ocean—
who wave and wave,
their backs to a breaking wave
held
in the split-second before it crashes around them,
the dull grey sheen of the sun
(unseen but felt) slanting even as it does now
on a jigsaw of boards and swollen pilings,
shops and tents and rides
closed tight, roped down,
covered over like expensive merchandise,
the ocean glittering as if
someone had been polishing it all night.

Globe/Elizabeth Spires

I spread my game on the cracked linoleum floor:
I had to play inside all day.
The woman who kept me said so.
She was middle-aged, drank tea in the middle of the day,
her face the color of dust layered on a table.

A high window let in alley light
to a two-room apartment.
Sofas and chairs bristled like hedgehogs
and made the backs of my legs itch.
No red flowers on the windowsill. No radio.
Just waxy vines drooping over the tables,
a dome clock dividing time into fifteen-minute parcels.

What did I do all day?
Made card houses so frail
I had to turn my breath the other way.
Or colored the newspaper comic strips,
or wobbled across the floor in my mother's old pumps
with the aplomb of somebody drunk.

Enter my father at 5:15, dark and immediate,
finished with his shift at the factory.
He was hiding something behind his back.
He turned as I circled him,
keeping whatever it was out of sight.
<u>Close your eyes and hold out your hand—</u>
I touched a globe slotted on top for coins,
my hand shadowing the continents
like a cloud thousands of miles wide.
He put my finger over the state where we lived,
then handed me his loose change to fill the world up with.

Memory's false as anything, spliced in the wrong parts,
queerly jumping. But better than forgetting.
We walked out into the soft light of October, leaves
sticking to our shoes like gold paper.
I was four years old and he was twenty-five,
same age as I am writing this.

Tequila/Elizabeth Spires

I live in a stone house high in the mountains,
close to the stars . . .
                              Last night, a little lonely,
I went to the bar in the valley
where the regulars tell their stories,
one about a man with a runaway dog
who stood by his door each night calling
Tequila, Tequila. Nobody
knew how long his grief would last
or what he did when his house went dark.
Did he sit all night tipping
a bottle of tequila to his mouth,
legs wrapping the bottle in warmth
the way a shot of tequila
wraps the throat? Or did he sleep
like everyone else, holding his parts
close to himself like a dog? Nobody should
go near a man who wants to be
that lonely. Nobody does.
Bragging, I told them I'd go back
to any year in my life
and live it over. I lied
and said nothing had ever scared me.
They looked at me, all husbands and fathers.
The stars will blind you, they warned,
the ghosts in the alley
will blow smoke in your eyes and steal
your money. I nodded, pretending to know.
But someday I'll leave this place with
only as much as I can carry,
taking the only road
out of the valley, the one that leads
everywhere. And though I'm not friendly,
I'll leave a note on the door,
black writing on a white square, cryptic
and small, so the regulars can make up
my story: Gone to find Tequila—

& What If/Terry Stokes

& what if my only sleep is another cold shoulder?
& what if the photograph of me reveals the poison
of my breath? & what if

there is a rainbow trout at the end of this line,
I throw it in my creel, take it home, & present it
to the dead brown cat.

What if there are great stories about how
I have handled my wives, how I appear to walk around
with my hands tied, how I lie about the weather
& its fallout.

& what if someone kills me this December morning
because I am stupid, attractive, un-willing
to bend over backwards like a cockroach in pain,
training for the minor Olympics of bliss.

& what if I lean a little more to the left,
& something worse than death finds its way
into my already creepy life, & gets cruel
with my last few surly bones.

& what if I am not even sure I want to walk
into a pharmacy, & buy a thousand prophylactics,
& invent some way to use them in this blinding storm.
& what if my only other accomplice is dead-tired

& holds an old child of ours at arms-length,
& shoves the meticulous breast into his mouth,
& he wakes-up a slow learner on my long boat
taking a short summer course to catch up

with the grief. & I find I must remind him
I love him, & he scoffs, my sun-burned tulip,
this simple flower I have been meaning for years.

If It's All The Same To You/Terry Stokes

I'm out of sorts. I'm sort of scared
of losing my only child. I wouldn't lose
him in a crowd of strangers; his chuckle
will bounce off any human being. I waited

until I was sure I was losing myself,
& then this short woman's belly started
to blow-up like a string of lies. Surprise.
You were already telling yourself one-liners

to amuse yourself; to kill time.
& I thought to myself quite often:
What a ball of wax. What a bunch of yarns
she must have hidden in there.

In the delivery room, I bathed you,
& your blue flesh warmed, & you smiled,
& I cried, & I've been madly in love
ever since. You are the good, sweet side

of my face. You are the figure who attracts
thousands of strangers, & teaches them
love is the set-up, the kicker. Love is
cracking-up for no apparent reason. I live

in this house without your comedy. It is like
being lost in a world of one's own sad creation.
If I were stronger I would locate a good
cosmetic surgeon; find a large reflecting pool,

& dive, & stroke until I was absolutely sure
I would never rise. I would babble, drool,
& with a little luck totally lose sight
of myself. & perhaps, you will use

the few words I can still spit out.
& son, sing them with your whole heart.
Now, here's how it starts.

/Terry Stokes

"There were woods in the back, and on one
side of the house. Therefore, it was happy childhood"

It was a cold childhood surrounded by
all those lousy trees. My father
lived in the midwest; he moved in a hurry
just before I was born.

It was the only job available. My mother
carried me, & she wanted to see
what kind of stuff he was made of. My mother
& I stayed around for two months, crying

most of the time. My father thought
about suicide. It didn't make
for a pleasing two o'clock feeding.
I didn't miss him eventhough I suppose

I was supposed to. My mother wanted him
to disappear from the face of the earth.
So, she brought me to this town without a river,
but there are plenty of serene trees.

My fathers pop in & out like groundhogs.
They smile at me; they bring me things
to toy with. They want my mother, of course,
& they get her. My first father

was buried last year in a pile
of rotting leaves. He froze-up,
his starter motor conked-out
on an unlit road. He tried to walk

the rest of the way; he lay down
for one of those moments
that seems to last forever.
No one taught me to miss him,

& I don't. I won't miss anything
that's wrapped-up in a skimpy coat
of leaves. I didn't even know
the tree. I'm not heartless;

I hate the wolf spiders here,
& I like to be held, & fussed over.
Fathers are a dime a dozen; mothers
come at the drop of a hat. I run

to the door, & sometimes I answer
when I am called for some unexplained reason.

The Nooning/Stephanie S. Tolan

Brine, simmering on the stove,
sends orders—
insistent, steamy hands
that draw me
through the breathless sunlight
to the center of the day.

But near the door
a shadow figure,
cool and dark,
beckons,
insistent too,
and I follow
to a world of night
lit by a silent, amber moon
where strange fishes dive
through transparent purple air
and wave the silken banners
of their tails
in the shimmer
of their moonspun foam.

I stand on a stone ledge
watching the fishes,
watching the shadow figure
angle a line
tipped with barbed hook
upward
into the froth of their passing.

He flings the line,
reels in,
flings and reels
until the stone beside him
reflects the moon
and his own dark shape.

Always the fishes pass,
weave and dive,
and the air gleams
as the line returns.
The moon slips
and slowly sets
beyond the solid stone
and I return

to the brine,
to the beans and beets,
the herbs and gleaming jars,
the August sun.

I return,
slowly,
to the steaming
center of the day.

Lunch/Stephanie S. Tolan

The children
(all boys)
sit around my table
moving constant forks and paper cups,
pushing at this motherhood
I wear like a trick-or-treat ghost.

The ceiling
with its painted sun
drops a food
when I glance at my plate
and the children stand,
wiping rubber mouths.

I glare the ceiling into place,
adjust eyeholes
and watch
four t-shirts disappear
through the closing door.

Upon the sticky table top
I lay my head a moment
before examining my paper bag
for treats.

Two Saints/Leonard Trawick

Two saints were conversing in heaven.

"And what were you in your former existence, madam?"

"I was a great chestnut tree. In spring as my buds opened
I strewed the earth with the sticky brown tabs which had
protected my tender leaves all winter. Then I bloomed into
a candelabra of candelabras and tossed down a froth of tiny
white flowers, each flecked with purple. All summer long
squirrels played among my boughs, nipping off twigs, which
I could easily spare. Soon my fruit began to swell, two or
three to a stem, and before long the shiny brown chestnuts
began to patter down through my leaves. With the nuts, the
burrs, too, fell—little vegetable hedgehogs, each dividing
into three spiked elf-sandals, dragons' tongues, instruments
for a fairy torture chamber. And the woody stems that had
held the flowers and fruit—toy sharp-tailed horses with
limbs awry—came tumbling after. As the days grew short and
cool, my leaves turned a brilliant yellow and fluttered to
my feet in a golden drift. Last, the stems of the leaves,
knitting needles of my summer garment, dropped away. Yet
already new sticky buds were swelling on the upturned tips
of my branches, preparing to burst open once again when
winter was past. And what were you, sir, previously?"

"Madam, what an extraordinary coincidence! I was gardener
for the very yard in which you grew! I raked up after you
all God-damned year!"

A Little Jug Music/Leonard Trawick

I

In Jugtown on Saturday night
Neat fifths and gallons all come out;
Tales go round of flagons smashed—
Jeroboam murmurs, "glass is frail";
Old Crock and Jorum debate which
Came first, the liquor or the keg.
What is the world but one vast jug?
What is a man but a jug of jugs?
Each sounds its clank or tinkle—
Barrels of bullet, pipes of amber song
Pour out all evening till they drop
Stained, reeking, void—drunk dead.

II

Late, when the East wind blows,
The jugs turn up their mouths and moan
Of bottles etched to rainbows
Under the silent mud,
Of demijohns dreaming corn whiskey,
And sunken amphoras like great crusted tears.
"Our burden was mirth and oblivion;
Who are we, now our work is done?"
The moaning is pleasant; it laves
The sides and tickles old resonances.
Strange, the full notes come
Only when the wine is gone.

III

Hoot, Toot, Honk, and Rump
Got drunk and landed in the dump.
"All-powerful Booze!" they cried,
"Was it for this that we endured
The kiln, the funnel, and the cork?—
Stood steadfast on the shelf,
And never leaked or splashed?"
"O Jugs," the mighty spirit said,
"Your bodies are but dross,
And destined for the long fill;
Yet every shape, inspired, will speak its name,
Which is itself and its eternal fame."

IV

Ain't gonna tote, ain't gonna hoe,
Tell the captain, ain't gonna go;
Pick my daisies where they grow:
Hoot, toot, honk, rump.

Everybody, Here's my name—
When I'm There, it's still the same;
Fun's my study, Now's my game;
Hoot, toot, honk, rump.

Fling butt, sing, stomp,
Scream, steam, squeeze, thump—
That's what we call the Jugtown jump:
Hoot, toot, honk, rump.

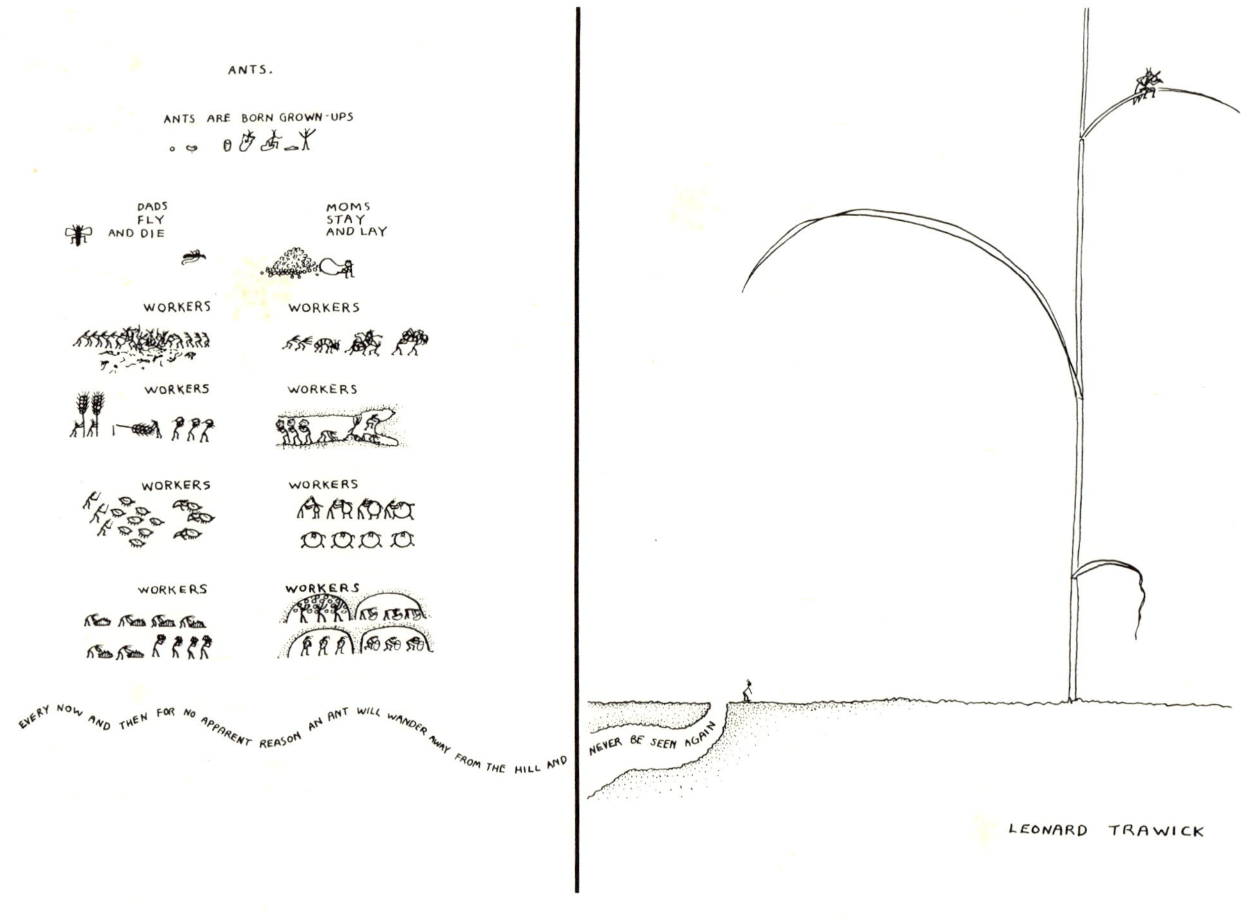
ANTS.
ANTS ARE BORN GROWN-UPS
DADS FLY AND DIE
MOMS STAY AND LAY
WORKERS
WORKERS
WORKERS
WORKERS
WORKERS
WORKERS
WORKERS
WORKERS
EVERY NOW AND THEN FOR NO APPARENT REASON AN ANT WILL WANDER AWAY FROM THE HILL AND
NEVER BE SEEN AGAIN
LEONARD TRAWICK

SUNDAY MORNINGS

LONG AGO, WHEN POPEYE FELT

AND THE BLUE GOON SAID,

AND INTO SWEE' PEA'S MIND FLASHED

THEN

AND GEEZIL SLUNK OFF MUTTERING   # @   !!

—MY DADDY READ THE FUNNIES SO

(EVEN WHEN HIS BREATH   )

—HE WAS   , IT WAS REALLY   !

AND EVEN NOW, THOUGH MY DAYS   ,

MY BREAD   , AND MY BEER   ,

IN SPITE OF   ,   , AND   ,

WHEN I OPEN THOSE SUNDAY FUNNIES,   !

IT'S   JUST

LEONARD TRAWICK

The Devil/Alberta Turner

While his crib still had sides   he woke screaming
arms beating   as if he'd been dropped

Found it easy to bite off
stems   bits of skin   spit them out
But numbers came wrong   Three apples
take away three left three cores

When he blew on a grass blade
no one came   When he caught a finch
he squeezed too hard

He enjoyed fire   Ears wrinkled   hair hissed
But his own finger hurt

Old Clootie   Teaser   Lad
Lurk in a pocket   lurk behind the Cross
take the hindmost   beat your wife
behind the door with a leg of lamb

Your special shoes   your forked sock
Your bedpost   paintbrush   darning needle   apron
your young   your milk

And all you know of falling is that dream

The Prudence of Nan Corbett/Alberta Turner

I didn't know which would work   so I tried
them all   Savings and loan   Savings and Trust
early Mass   salt over my shoulder   In spring
I poured cider on the plow

But winter came anyhow
A hare sucked my cow dry   my hens got roup
my fur went bald   my battery died

This year I really tried
I asked for Gene at the Full Service Island
butchered the pig in the waxing moon
and when a black dog tried to lead me home
with him I threw a bone in front of the dog

But winter came
My feet went through the Chevy's floor
I forgot to tell the bees and they swarmed away
I got the roup   my tractor lamed

So much for luck   Next year I'll make sure
have my spleen and my appendix out
spit twice when I harness a white horse
rustproof the Chevy   and on Christmas Eve
I'll spread fresh straw   shut the stable door
and won't look

Knees/Alberta Turner

So much to touch
I've let my fingers laze
mittened them to mere spoons
So many wires to twist and skeins to tease

So many lean things
climb   swing   hang
roll down long slopes of gravel and gorse
give birth again

And fat blunt things
used soap   used stone
chins in hands
thumbs

If Death complains
I'll say   Don't grieve
You're the drum
I thump my knee on
gong   bell   belfry
of knees

Confederate Sharpshooter at Devil's Den /James Ulmer

after a photograph by Mathew Brady

I remember this photograph
from my sixth grade history book—
when the teacher wasn't looking
I would turn to it and stare.
That spring we went to Gettysburg
and a guide showed us the mass graves
where the unrecognizable dead
had been heaped. The stone markers
read Pennsylvania, Virginia, New York,
and I thought I saw, under
trimmed grass, the jumble of arms and legs.
In the museum I saw the photograph again,
read how it was taken
three days after the battle in summer heat.
Brady's assistants dragged the body over rocks,
positioned it right, musket by the still hand.
They turned the head partly away,
a gesture, perhaps, in deference
to the enemy they didn't hate.
What if a young wife from Georgia
saw the picture and recognized, in the swollen face,
the features that had been her husband's,
that she had turned to so often
at night. I imagine
the clatter of tripods, dust, flies buzzing,
the men in their vests and shirt sleeves
holding kerchiefs over their mouths.

These Nights/James Ulmer

the full moon drains me.
White roses below my window

seem about to rise from their stems,
confused by so much light.

The shadows of streetlamps
describe a ladder I keep trying

to climb, hoping for ease. But gravity
holds me now. I walk our rooms:

leaded windows, brass doorknobs, ornaments
of coming and going. You wanted

to live here surrounded by roses, hornets
droning, the blossoms lasting

into winter—all this ruined now
by your absence. The time

you read my cards the five of cups
turned up—three cups spilled, two full—

and you warned me not to mourn.
Now the rooms swirl with a faint

dust, or pollen, in which my steps
leave no trace. I remember now

your breasts lifted and fell as you slept,
my uncertain ground, partly in shadow,

partly in light—How the moon
weaves through these blinds! Often

you would murmur in your sleep,
and I would lean close to listen.

leave no trace. I remember how

Swimmer in the Rain/Robert Wallace

No one but him
seeing the rain
start—a fine scrim
far down the bay,
smoking, advancing
between two grays
till the salt-grass rustles
and the creek's mirror
in which he stands
to his neck, like clothing
cold, green, supple,
begins to ripple.

The drops bounce up,
little fountains
all around him,
swift, momentary—
every drop tossed back
in air atop
its tiny column—
glass balls balancing
upon glass nipples,
lace of dimples,
a stubble of silver
stars, eye-level,
incessant, wild.

White, dripping, tall,
ignoring the rain,
an egret fishes
in the creek's margin,
dips to the minnows'
sky, under which,
undisturbed, steady
as faith the tide pulls.
Mussels hang
like grapes on a piling.
Wet is wet.

The swimmer settles
to the hissing din—
a glass bombardment,
parade of diamonds,
blinks, jacks of light,
wee Brancusi's, chromes
like grease-beads sizzling,
myriad—and swims
slowly, elegantly,
climbing tide's ladder
hand over hand
toward the distant bay.

Hair and eye-brows
streaming, sleek crystal
scarving his throat—
no one but him.

Everything Comes Eventually/Robert Wallace

As, today, May's shirtsleeve air,
dogs, jonquils, girls,
sunlit past seven o'clock; or

as, in time, the first snow rasping
brown oak leaves.
Love, too. And the end of it.

Girl In An Apartment Window/Robert Wallace

At my sink, I'm running
water for coffee.

A Degas lit in brick,
your window

shows you lifting your gown
over your head,

torso, breasts in the light.
You gather

it like a cloud, bend,
vanish, come

back buttoning a shirt,
tossing

hair outside the collar.
Then, other

windows become other poses.
In one you're

by a table, looking down,
cup in hand.

Truce/Laura Wallencheck

For my life, I could not make out
your words, and mine made you laugh,
reluctant, the laugh creasing the wariness
in your eyes. At each little foxhole
in the conversation we rested from the stealth
of picking between the wineglasses
to the frontiers of our words.
But when home looked a better hold for me
than foreign places, what saved me from retreat
was the white token of your touch and
that low croon of yours that I remembered
from before learning words.

/Laura Wallencheck

There's an art to cutting glass.
First a score, not how
but where; not deep,
just there,
complete from edge
to edge.
What's left—and here's
the art—
is the sharp snap
down, believing
that the glass
knows what
to do.

In My Place/Laura Wallencheck

I heard where you were
last night; I have my spies.
Your group sat pulled up
to the table, working
the conversation
to make it sound just right,
brittle as the cheap glasses
before you, but with
smooth edges.
More women than men, she said,
and I see your bright confusion.
I worry about the strays.
I wonder whose ankle you were
catching under the table.

Chasing the Word/Cameron Webster

My rainhat is on.
Coat buttoned and belted.
I will head down Clement
to a bar, look
for something that should
be here.

If I find it there,
will I care?
Will it fool me this time?

The brim of my rainhat
slants across my forehead
like a scar.

early morning on the common/Cameron Webster

suddenly I am at the window
the slap of a dream in my ears
moist lips still on my eyes

everything out there on the common
drifts like green whispers
a bird rides a branch like
the end of a whip
and you move, radiant in your
nakedness, frightened wings
flickering in your black hair

you step lightly
careful not to disturb
a thing with your toes
and you rise on them
twirl like the only
whirlwind in the world
then you are gone

I turn back to the darkness
and whisper that you
were the most beautiful breeze

The Intruder/Cameron Webster

She is in her bedroom with me
but I feel someone else taking her
small breasts into his mouth
I punch a hole in the wall
and reach for him in there
but he slips away.

We sit at a bar and he's there again
looking out of the wine grotesquely
with tongue extended
the glass
shatters in my hand
sending slivers through
the yellow fat to bone.

We drive towards the sea
and he is thrusting deeply with her
her eyes pressed like smooth
sea shells into her head—I reach
into her hair
cup the bone like living sea water
and know,
finally,
that I hold them there together,
and I can take my hand away.

Down by the Salley Gardens/Dallas Wiebe

Downwind,
I called my cuckoo to love
In the valley
    of the sad gardens
Where the willows
    hang down their heads
And the lilacs and the iris
Sop up the spring rains.
She scowled
        as she removed her wooden eyes,
        her tin lips
        and her leaden ears.
She recoiled in the cold wind.
She vowed
She could not stand for me.
I told her I loved her
        in my deepest basso profundo
And laid her down
In the grasp of carefree time.
When she wept
I withdrew behind the sodden oaks.
Darkness fell on our parting.
The white ducks came
        and nibbled away my beauty.
Now I am one and twenty
And the wisemen
        have to come to Bethlehem,
        tripping on the dead Palestinians,
        and saying,
"Where is he
Who is king of kings
And Lord of Lords?
Where is he whose countenance
        is as the sun?"

The University Poet/Dallas Wiebe

He was born with catarrh,
    scrofula and terminal unction.
His father absconded
    with the umbilicus
    after oxygen ate his baby's brains.
His mother weaned him
    at two seconds.
He grew up
    under a cloud of ticks.
In high school
    he played tailback
    in the shower.
In college he studied
    calumny, deceit-and scurrility.
He has degrees
    from thermometers, burns and crime.

His poems fly off
    at public expense.
Promotions fall like dead pigeons
    into his shorts.
He thinks the eagle of art
    has carried him
    into a struggle with time.

When he fingers his blank pages,
Box elders die,
Rabbits cover their ears
And horses run
    from their mares.

To My Valentine/Dallas Wiebe

That dirigible that flew up your nose
Was a decent, gentle thought from me to you.
That elephant you swallowed
Was a happy, pleasant greeting from yours truly.
That telephone pole I stuck in your ear
Was my way of saying "I love you."

You bubble-headed bitch, I could kick you
For your sweet way of saying "Hi."
You miserable creep, I could lick you
For calling me "Honey."
You ugly fathead, I could beat you
For your funereal stroke.

Your odors excite me.
Your droppings intrigue me.
Your vomit fascinates me.
Your ideas amuse me.
It's your presence that bothers me.

That tornado in the parlor
Is me leaving.
That volcano on the lawn
Is my departing dust.
That drab fire around the heavens
Is my last wish for you.

My Love is Like/Dallas Wiebe

Her face is more fishy
Than an ocean looking for water.
Her hands are more soiled
Than a Kansas farm.
She's as gentle
As a dead cow.

She asks,
"Why have I asked? And when?
And if not her, whom?"
Because my lust is as trivial
As a crossroads.
And she has never walked
Under a pendulum.

Someday I'll touch her terrific hands.
Somewhere I'll feel her enormous ideas.
Somehow I'll speak without words.
Because she knows
I'm as cynical as a dog,
My ideas are as cold as a broken record
And my skin is stone.

Elegy in the Form of an Invitation/David Young

James Wright b. 1927, Martin's Ferry, Ohio;
d. 1980, New York City.

Early spring in Ohio. Lines
of thunderstorms, quiet flares
on the southern horizon.
A doctor stares at his hands.
His friend the schoolmaster
plays helplessly with a thread.

I know you have put your voice aside
and entered something else.

I like to think you could come back here now
like a man returning to his body
after a long dream of pain and terror.

It wouldn't all be easy:
sometimes the wind blows birds
right off their wires and branches,
chemical wastes smolder on weedy sidings,
codgers and crones still starve in shacks
in the hills above Portsmouth and Welfare . . .
hobo, cathouse, slagheap, old mines
that never exhaust their veins—
it is all the way you said.

But there is this fierce green
and bean shoots poking through potting soil
and in a month or so the bees
will move like sparks among the roses.

And I like to think
the things that hurt won't hurt you anymore
and that you will come back
in the spring, for the quiet,
the dark shine of grackles,
raccoon tracks by the river,
the moon's ghost in the afternoon,
and the black earth behind the plowing.

Russell Atkins

is a Cleveland native and a widely respected poet and composer. He has been a consultant for educational TV, a poet in the schools and a writer in residence at many colleges and universities. In addition to being invited to Bread Loaf and having his work introduced at Darmstadt's Avant-garde Music Festival (Germany), he received an honorary doctorate from Cleveland State University. His poems have appeared in many magazines and have been widely anthologized. His collections include Phenomena, Objects, Here In The, Whichever and Heretofore, distributed by Benjamin Blom, Inc.

"While Waiting for A Friend To Come Visit A Friend In A Mental Hospital," "Football Practice In Woodland Haven," from Here In The, Cleveland State University Poetry Center, © 1976 Russell Atkins; "Lakefront, Cleveland," from Heretofore, Paul Breman Publishers, © 1968 Russell Atkins, originally appeared in EXPERIMENT 1958.

John M. Bennett

holds a Ph.D. in Latin American poetry from UCLA and has published articles and books on the subject. Among his poetry collections are Nips Poems, Meat Watch, Burning Dog, Blender and Some Blood (joint poems written with C. Mehrl Bennett). His work as a literary experimentalist has led to numerous publications and exhibitions. He is Head of Luna Bisonte Prods, which publishes books, other poetry products and a magazine, LOST AND FOUND TIMES.

"No Matter," and "no soap," from Blender, Ghost Dance Press, © 1983 John M. Bennett, ("No Matter" originally appeared in LOST AND FOUND TIMES and IMPOSSIBILITIES; "no soap" appeared as a postcard from Press Me Close); "No," ORIGINAL ART MAGAZINE, © 1982 John M. Bennett.

James Bertolino

has received a number of prizes and awards, including the Discovery Award, the Book-of-the-Month Club Prize Fellowship and a National Endowment for the Arts writers fellowship. Since 1968 14 collections of his poetry have been published—the most recent and most comprehensive are New & Selected Poems, 1978, Carnegie—Mellon University Press, and Precinct Kali & The Gertrude Spicer Story, 1982, New Rivers Press. He received an MFA from Cornell University in 1973 and since 1974 has been a professor of English at the University of Cincinnati.

"The Woman Who Collaborates," ARTFUL DODGE, © 1982 James Bertolino; "Beware The Roses" © 1983 James Bertolino; and "The Cocoon," INDIANA REVIEW, © 1983 James Bertolino.

Laurel Blossom

"Under the Covers," POETRY, © 1982 Laurel Blossom; "Leaving," from Any Minute, Greenhouse Review Press, © 1979 Laurel Blossom, originally appeared in POETRY; "Habitforming," © 1983 Laurel Blossom.

Phil Boiarski

"Unexposed," "Secrets," © 1983 Phil Boiarski.

Imogene L. Bolls

is a native of Kansas who has also lived in the West and is a professor of English at Wittenberg University in Springfield. Her poems have appeared in more than 75 literary periodicals and anthologies, including PRAIRIE SCHOONER, THE TEXAS REVIEW, MISSISSIPPI REVIEW, PLAINS POETRY JOURNAL and HIRAM POETRY REVIEW. Her chapbook, Glass Walker, was published in 1983 by the Cleveland State University Poetry Center. In addition to the OAC fellowship, she has been awarded summer study grants in 1980 and 1982 enabling her to work with Hopi song poets in northern Arizona.

"Ohio Spring Storm," © 1983 Imogene L. Bolls; "The Dream," from Glass Walker, Cleveland State University Press, © 1983 Imogene L. Bolls; "Deer Watching in Frijoles Canyon," IMAGES, © 1982 Imogene L. Bolls; "In Retrospect: Oedipus to the Sphinx," THE GEORGIA REVIEW, © 1969 Imogene L. Bolls.

Grace Butcher

is an associate professor of English at the Geauga campus of Kent State University and has been a national champion in track. She still competes in track as well as motor-cycle racing (touring and street riding) and writes a monthly column on bikes for RIDER Magazine. She has been a poet since age 11 and has been performing her work in schools and on radio and TV since the early 1960s. Her most recent poetry collections are Rumors of Ecstasy . . . Rumors of Death and Before I Go Out On the Road.

"Responsibilities," "New and Old Beginnings," "Day Full of Rustling Murmuring Lies," from Before I Go Out On the Road,

Cleveland State University Poetry Center, © 1979 Grace Butcher. ("Responsibilities" first appeared in 73 Ohio Poets, Cornfield Review Press, 1978). "Wife of the Moon Man Who Never Came Back," from Rumors of Ecstasy . . . Rumors of Death, Ashland Poetry Press, © 1971 Grace Butcher, reprinted by Barnwood Press, 1981, originally appeared in HIRAM POETRY REVIEW.

Anne Chamberlain

was born and raised in Marietta, attended Marietta College and the University of Cincinnati, and has resettled in Marietta after living in New York City for many years. She is the author of three novels published in the U.S. and England: The Tall Dark Man, The Soldier Room and The Darkest Bough. Her poems and stories have appeared in many magazines.

"Hospital Visit," The Columbus Citizen-Journal, © 1979 Anne Chamberlain.

Hale Chatfield

is a member of the faculty at Hiram College in Hiram, Ohio, and is founder of the HIRAM POETRY REVIEW. His articles, poems and stories have appeared in many magazines and anthologies. He has had five volumes of poetry published: The Young Country and Other Poems (1959), Teeth (1967), At Home (1971), What Color Are Your Eyes? (1978), and Water Colors (1979). His most recent book is a collection of short fiction: Little Fictions, Loving Lies (1981). He has received grants and fellowships from the National Endowment for the Humanities and the National Endowment for the Arts. From 1968 to 1972, he served as co-chairman of the first literature advisory panel of the Ohio Arts Council.

"The Wolf," from Attention Please, © 1976 by Hearthstone Press, reprinted by permission.

Sister Maryanna Childs

has been a Domincan Sister of St. Mary of the Springs, Columbus, since 1930. She has taught creative writing at Ohio Dominican College since 1945, and has published 8 books, and 300 poems, 42 stories, and 65 articles in some 40 religious and secular periodicals in the past 50 years.

"Short Story," THE LYRIC, © 1982 Sister Maryanna Childs; "The Wise Cow's Tale," LIGUORIAN, © 1980 Sister Maryanna Childs.

David Citino

is a native of Cleveland and has degrees from Ohio University and The Ohio State University. Currently he is an associate professor of English at The Ohio State University at Marion where he edits the CORNFIELD REVIEW and is also poetry editor for THE OHIO JOURNAL. His poems have appeared in numerous periodicals including THE BELOIT POETRY JOURNAL, BENNINGTON REVIEW, CHICAGO REVIEW, SHENANDOAH and YALE REVIEW. His collections are Last Rites and Other Poems (Ohio State University Press, 1980) and The Appassionata Poems (Cleveland State University Poetry Center, 1983).

"Sister Mary Appasionata Lectures the Religion and Mythology Classes: Frogs & Foreskins, Heart and Tongue," and "Sister Mary Appassionata Lectures the Neurology Class," from The Appassionata Poems," The Cleveland State University Poetry Center, © 1983 David Citino; "Thomas Alva Edison Writes to Madame Elena Blavatsky, 1878," SHENANDOAH, © 1981 David Citino.

Marian Clover

is a freelance writer living in Columbus. She has published over 300 articles, short stories and poems, one chapbook and, in collaboration, a book of poetry/photography.

"Cloudbank," © 1983 Marian Clover; "Craftsman," KANSAS QUARTERLY, © 1976 Marian Clover; "Architecture," REVIEW 76, © 1976 Marian Clover.

Horace Coleman

is a native Ohioan with roots in the Cherokee/Chickasaw peoples as well as direct African ancestry. His poems have appeared in such periodicals as IOWA REVIEW, GREENFIELD REVIEW, AMERICAN POETRY REVIEW and NEW LETTERS, and have been anthologized in Contemporary Poetry From A to Z, Peace is Our Profession, Demilitarized Zones, and Between A Rock & A Hard Place (BkMk Press). He has read his work on a variety of radio programs including "At the Arabica" and "New Letters On the Air."

"How I Know It's Over," "At Pemaquid Point" and "No Sweat Vet," © 1983 Horace W. Coleman, Jr.

Wayne Dodd

is a professor of English at Ohio University and editor of the OHIO REVIEW. His poems have appeared in many periodicals. His most recent book is The Names You

<u>Gave It</u>, Louisiana State University Press, 1980.

"Of Butterflies," THE GEORGIA REVIEW, © 1981 Wayne Dodd; "Danny's Uncle," <u>The Names You Gave It</u>, Louisiana State University Press, © 1980 Wayne Dodd.

Leatrice W. Emeruwa

is a Cleveland native with degrees from Howard and Kent State universities. She is an assistant professor at the Metropolitan Campus of Cuyahoga Community College and specializes in black literature and creative writing. Her poems have appeared in numerous periodicals and she is the author of a poetry collection: <u>Black Girl, Black Girl</u>, and a play, <u>Black Magic—Anyone?</u>

"We Knew the Signs," from <u>Ev'ry Shut Eye Ain't Sleep; Ev'ry Goodbye Ain't Gone,</u> © 1977 Leatrice W. Emeruwa; "The Jesus Lady," © 1980 Leatrice W. Emeruwa.

Barbara Fialkowski

directs the MFA program in creative writing at Bowling Green State University. In addition to publishing in many periodical publications, she is the author of a chapbook from Croissant & Co.

"From Here," © 1983 Barbara Fialkowski McMillen.

Robert Flanagan

is the author of <u>Maggot,</u> a novel, and poetry collections <u>The Full Round</u>, and <u>Once You Learn You Never Forget</u>. His poems and stories have appeared recently in OHIO REVIEW, OHIO JOURNAL, and CHICAGO REVIEW. He lives in Delaware where he is a professor of English at Ohio Wesleyan University.

"The Gambler In Love," and "A Prophet of Loss," © 1983 Robert Flanagan; "Circus," from <u>Once You Learn You Never Forget</u>, Fiddlehead Books, © 1978 Robert Flanagan.

Stuart Friebert

directs the writing program at Oberlin College where he is also co-editor of FIELD. He has published 10 collections of poetry, most recently <u>Uncertain Health</u>. He has also co-translated three collections of translations and has recently co-edited with David Young <u>The Longman Anthology of Contemporary American Poetry: 1950-1980</u>.

"Submarine Poem" from <u>Uncertain Health,</u> Woolmer & Brotherson, © 1979 Stuart Friebert; "For Our Retarded Brothers," SHENANDOAH, © 1981 Stuart Friebert.

Marilyn Gravett

"Palm Sunday Tornado, 1964," "Running Things Backward," and "Menses," © 1983 Marilyn Gravett.

Terry Hermsen

a Michigan native, has remained in Ohio since graduating from Wittenberg University. He currently lives in the country outside Plymouth. His poems have appeared in such periodicals as DESCANT, HIRAM POETRY REVIEW, THE HUMANIST, ILLINOIS QUARTERLY and PIG IRON. He is very active in the writing component of the Ohio Arts Council's Artists in Education Program and in the fall of 1982 was poet in residence for the city of Springfield. An avid bicyclist, he is currently working on a book of poems about bicycling across the U.S.

"Lives of the Tribes," originally appeared in CINCINNATI POETRY REVIEW, © 1982 Terry Hermsen; "12 Proverbs," © 1983 Terry Hermsen; "Call in the Night," from <u>The Story of Ordinary Poetry: American poetry of the 1970s</u>, Savelli Editions, © 1982 Terry Hermsen.

Robert Hudzik

is a librarian at the Cincinnati Public Library. His poems have appeared in many magazines including CINCINNATI POETRY REVIEW, HIRAM POETRY REVIEW and SLOW LORIS. His work was included in the recent anthology <u>Five Cincinnati Poets</u>.

"The Tunnel," WATERS, © 1978 Robert Hudzik; "The Animals Within," POETRY NORTHWEST, © 1973 Robert Hudzik; "Self-Portrait With Glasses," POET LORE, © 1982 Robert Hudzik.

James C. Kilgore

is a professor of English at the Cuyahoga Community College in Cleveland. A native of Louisiana, he is a veteran of military service with the Army in Italy, Austria and Germany during the Second World War, and has read his poetry at colleges and universities across the country. His poems, essays and stories have appeared in such periodicals as BLACK WORLD, PHYLON, PRAIRIE SCHOONER and OBSIDIAN. His eighth collection, <u>African Violet: Poem for a Black Woman,</u> was published in 1982.

"Until I Met You," "No Ordinary Beginnings," and "An Awkward Silence," from <u>African Violet: Poem For A Black Woman,</u> Lotus Press, © 1982 James C. Kilgore.

Joel Lipman

is a Wisconsin native who has lived in Toledo since 1975. He teaches English and creative writing at the University of Toledo where he co-founded The Toledo Poets Center with Nick Muska. The translitics published in this book are loosely based on Spanish poems by Julian del Casal and Herberto Padilla, and are part of a book-length manuscript in preparation. His two collections are <u>Mercury Vapor Lamp</u> (Ocooch Mountain Press, 1980) and <u>Chicago You Got A Wide Stance</u> (Piirto Press, 1981). His visual language designs have been widely published and exhibited, and are available, along with his books, from The Colony Bookstore & Gallery, 2214 West Central Avenue, Toledo, Ohio 43606.

"The Real Ideal," WHITE PINE JOURNAL, © 1983 Joel Lipman; "Sir Walter Raleigh Goes to the Movies" and two visuals, © 1983 Joel Lipman.

Howard McCord

was born in El Paso and has lived in Bowling Green since 1970 when he assumed directorship of the MFA program in creative writing at Bowling Green State University. He is a long distance runner, a sharpshooter, and has hiked in the Alaskan ice flats as well as in the West. He is the author of 23 books, including <u>Selected</u> <u>Poems</u> from The Crossing Press. His most recent book is a collection of prose, <u>Walking Edges,</u> from Raincrow Press in Ohio.

"Old Habits," "Directions" and "Off A Bit," © 1983 Howard McCord.

Robert McGovern

was born in Minneapolis and was educated at the universities of Minnesota and London, and Case Western Reserve University, from which he holds a Ph.D. He has taught at Radford University, Virginia, and has been professor of English and creative writing at Ashland College for the past 18 years. His poetry and criticism have appeared in THE NATION, KANSAS QUARTERLY, ZEITGEIST, BLUE UNICORN and many other periodicals here and abroad. His two books in print are a poetry collection, <u>A Feast of Flesh and Other Occasions,</u> and <u>A Poetry Ritual for Grammar Schools</u> (a handbook for elementary teachers), available from The Ashland Poetry Press, Ashland College, Ashland, Ohio 44805.

"Light At the Beginning of the Tunnel," FORUM, Ball State University, © 1975 Robert McGovern.

William McLaughlin

has a B.A. from Western Reserve University and an M.S. from the University of Wisconsin. He has taught government, economics and physical geography for the past 26 years in Cleveland and has traveled extensively in Ireland, England, Spain, and Yugoslavia. He is also a fiction writer and a playwright and was a fellow at the Midwest Playwrights' Laboratory in 1977 at the University of Wisconsin. His poems have appeared in numerous periodicals; his most recent collection is <u>At Rest in the Midwest</u> published by the Cleveland State University Poetry Center in 1982.

"Ice On the Pond," PRAIRIE SCHOONER, © 1982 William McLaughlin; "Siting," THE CHOWDER REVIEW, © 1983 William McLaughlin; "Dornava Palace," THE DENVER QUARTERLY, © 1981 William McLaughlin.

William McMillen

has lived in Ohio since 1969 and received a Ph.D. in twentieth-century literature and creative writing from Ohio University. He has taught English full-time on the faculty of Bowling Green State University and worked in the Office of Continuing Education there as well. He is presently assistant to the president of the Medical College of Ohio in Toledo. He has published short stories and poems in many literary magazines and has had a full-length drama, <u>The Peacock Colony</u>, produced at Bowling Green State University.

"Four Portraits," © William McMillen.

Jack Matthews

has completed his most recent novel, <u>Sassafras,</u> which will be published by Houghton, Mifflin in the fall of 1983. His most recent collection of stories, <u>Dubious Persuasions</u>, is in its second printing with the Johns Hopkins University Press. He is distinguished professor of English at Ohio University.

"An Old Sportswriter Celebrates His Fiftieth Anniversary of Covering the Yale-Dartmouth Game," THE NEW REPUBLIC, © 1980 Jack Matthews; "The Instant" and

"That Poems Should be Printed On Recyclable Paper Is Only Right," POETRY, © 1982 Jack Matthews.

Nick Muska

is a native of Lorain and a graduate of Antioch College and the University of California, Santa Barbara. His poems have appeared in such magazines as THE CHICAGO REVIEW and THE LAST VILLAGE IDIOT. Currently, he coordinates the Toledo Poets Center with Joel Lipman and teaches in the TPC's Inmate Arts Program at two northwest Ohio correctional institutions. Nick's poems are collected in Elm: Warehouse Poems, and he has also edited a collection of inmate writing, From Inside Out. Both books are available from The Toledo Poet's Center, UH 507-C, Univ. of Toledo, Toledo, Ohio 43606.

"Sunset XII," "Sunset XIII, The Cherelles Live at The Monster, St. Valentine's Day," and "David Allan Coe Gives Key West A Free Street Concert," POET'S MOUTH, © 1982 Nick Muska.

Julie L. Miller

"Dawn—After the Argument," "What the Visiting Poet Said," and "It Happened In Slow Motion," © 1983 Julie C. Miller.

Jane Piirto Navarre

is a poet and fiction writer from the upper peninsula of Michigan. Her poems and stories have appeared in such publications as the SOUTH DAKOTA REVIEW, POETRY NOW and the DENVER QUARTERLY. She lives in Bowling Green where her Piirto Press publishes poetry postcards and chapbooks.

"Reverie," © 1983 Jane P. Navarre; "Runners," POETRY NOW, © 1983 Jane P. Navarre; "To A Sleeping Child," from mamamama, Piirto Press, © 1979 Jane P. Navarre, originally appeared in FIRELANDS ARTS REVIEW.

Gary Pacernick

is a professor of English at Wright State University, Dayton. His poems have appeared in many magazines, including POETRY NOW, AMERICAN POETRY REVIEW, NORTH AMERICAN REVIEW, MIDSTREAM and JUDAISM. His poems have been anthologized in such collections as Travelling America with Today's Poets, and Poems Within the Ark: Modern Jewish Poets. His verse play I Want to Write a Jewish Poem was produced at the Dayton Art Institute at Wright State, Brandeis University and on public television. He is the editor of the poetry tabloid, IMAGES.

"Story," THE NORTH AMERICAN REVIEW, © 1976 Gary Pacernick; "Babel," AMERICAN POETRY REVIEW, © 1979 Gary Pacernick; "The Air Force Museum," MID-ATLANTIC REVIEW, © 1975 Gary Pacernick; "Sandbox Burial," POETRY NOW, © 1982 Gary Pacernick.

Frank Polite

holds degrees from Youngstown State University and the State University of Iowa. He served in the U.S. Navy and has held a variety of jobs including teaching English here and abroad. His work has been published in many periodicals and is anthologized in The New Yorker Book of Poems and A Geography of Poets. Some of his poems are collected in Letters in Transit, from City Miner Press.

"The Last House in Luna Pier," © 1979 Frank Polite.

James Reiss

grew up in Washington Heights, a neighborhood in New York City, and was educated at the University of Chicago. For the past 20 years his work has appeared in such periodicals as THE AMERICAN POETRY REVIEW, ESQUIRE, THE KENYON REVIEW and THE NEW YORKER. His collections are The Breathers (Ecco Press, 1974), and Express, (University of Pittsburgh Press, 1983). He is also the editor of Self-Interviews: James Dickey. He has taught creative writing at Miami University since 1965 where he is a professor of English.

"The Green Tree," from The Breathers, Ecco Press, © 1974 James Reiss, originally appeared in the NEW AMERICAN REVIEW; "A Candy Store in Washington Heights," from Express, University of Pittsburgh Press, © 1983 James Reiss, originally appeared in ANTAEUS.

Michael J. Rosen

currently teaches poetry at the Ohio State University, and is active in the artists in education programs of the Ohio Arts Council and the Greater Columbus Arts Council. His poems are forthcoming or have appeared in THE ATLANTIC MONTHLY, THE NATION, PRAIRIE SCHOONER and THE NEW ENGLAND REVIEW, among other periodicals. He has received an Ingram Merrill Foundation Fellowship for his writing, as well as OAC awards, and is presently marketing a poetry collection entitled "A Drink at the Mirage."

"Making Scents," THE AGNI REVIEW, © 1980 Michael J. Rosen.

Joel Rudinger

is an associate professor of English and Humanities at the Firelands campus of Bowling Green State University in Huron. His magazine publications include the NEW YORK QUARTERLY, COLORADO NORTH REVIEW, CAPRICORN and ALASKA POETRY. His first poetry collection, First Edition: 40 poems is now out of print and he is presently circulating another manuscript.

"Solo I Will Stand In the Winds That Choose To Take Me," © 1983 Joel Rudinger; "Sitting For Margaret," FIRELANDS REVIEW, © 1980 Joel Rudinger.

Elizabeth Spires

grew up in Circleville and received a B.A. from Vassar College. She worked as an assistant editor for Charles Merrill Publishing in Columbus before moving to Baltimore, Maryland where she currently teaches at Goucher College. Her first collection, Globe, was published in 1981 by Wesleyan University Press. Her poems have appeared in such periodicals as THE NEW YORKER, THE NEW REPUBLIC, POETRY and PARIS REVIEW. In addition to an OAC fellowship, she has also received a fellowship from the National Endowment for the Arts.

"Boardwalk," "Globe" and "Tequila," from Globe, Wesleyan University Press, © Elizabeth Spires. Reprinted by permission of Wesleyan University Press. ("Globe" and "Boardwalk" originally appeared in POETRY; "Tequila" originally appeared in THE NEW YORKER.)

Terry Stokes

was born in New York and teaches at the University of Cincinnati. Twelve chapbook and full-length collections of his poetry have been published, the most recent of which are Issuing of Scars (Bartholomew's Cobble Press, 1981) and Life in These United States (St. Luke's Press, 1979). One collection of his short fiction, Intimate Apparel, was published by Release Press in 1980.

"& What If" and "If It's All the Same to You," CONFRONTATION, © 1981, 1978, Terry Stokes; "There Were Woods in the Back . . ." PARTISAN REVIEW, © 1981 Terry Stokes.

Stephanie Tolan

began her writing career as a playwright and poet, and in 1976 began writing novels for young readers. These novels are: Grandpa—And Me, The Last of Eden, The Liberation of Tansy Warner, No Safe Harbors, The Great Skinner Strike and A Time to Fly Free. Her books have won several awards including the Ohioana Book Award for Juvenile Literature.

"Lunch" and "The Nooning," © 1983 Stephanie S. Tolan.

Leonard Trawick

grew up in Alabama and now teaches English at Cleveland State University. He is an editor of the CSU Poetry Center and founding editor of THE GAMUT, a multi-disciplinary quarterly published by Cleveland State University. His poems have appeared in such periodicals as POETRY, QUARTERLY WEST, ANTIOCH REVIEW and CHICAGO REVIEW. His collections are a chapbook of emblem poems, Beast Forms, from CSU, and Severed Parts, (Bits Press, 1981).

"A Little Jug Music," "Two Saints" and visuals: "Ants" and "Sunday Mornings," © 1983 Leonard Trawick.

Alberta Turner

is a native of New York state who was educated at Hunter College, Wellesley, and the Ohio State University. She is presently director of the poetry center at Cleveland State University where she is a professor of English. Her last poetry collection is Learning to Count from the University of Pittsburgh Press, and a new collection, A Belfry of Knees, is forthcoming from the University of Alabama Press. She is presently a member of the Ohio Arts Council's Literature Advisory Panel.

"The Devil," "The Prudence of Nan Corbett," © 1983 Alberta Turner. "Knees" appeared previously in Seven + 7, Ohio Arts Council, © 1981 Alberta Turner. All three poems are forthcoming in A Belfry of Knees, to be published by the University of Alabama Press in 1983.

James Ulmer

is a native of Cincinnati and received an M.A. in creative writing from the University of Washington in 1981. The following year he was a Hoyns Fellow in poetry at the University of Virginia, and he is currently a

Cullen Fellow and a Ph.D. student in the writing program at the University of Houston. His poems have appeared in POETRY, POETRY NORTHWEST, CRAZY HORSE, THE MISSOURI REVIEW and other magazines.

"These Nights," CRAZY HORSE, © 1982 James Ulmer; "Confederate Sharpshooter at Devil's Den," SEATTLE REVIEW, © 1981 James Ulmer.

Robert Wallace

teaches at Case Western Reserve University. His most recent collection of poems is Swimmer in the Rain, Carnegie-Mellon University Press, 1979. He is the author of a textbook, Writing Poems, and is the editor of LIGHT YEAR '84, the first number of an annual of light verse and funny poems to be published by Bits Press.

"Girl In An Apartment Window," "Swimmer in the Rain," "Everything Comes Eventually," from Swimmer in the Rain, Carnegie-Mellon University Press, © 1979 Robert Wallace.

Laura Wallencheck

born in Cleveland, holds a B.A. in English literature from The Ohio State University. She is currently editor of the OAC's artspace and is preparing the final man-uscript of her first novel for publication.

"Truce," "Untitled" and "In My Place," © 1983 Laura Wallencheck.

Cameron Webster

is a Vermont native who is currently an English instructor at Bowling Green State University. His poems and stories have appeared in several magazines and anthologies, including TOUCHSTONE and AN OLD WAGS TALE.

"Chasing the Word," "early morning on the common" and "The Intruder," © 1983 Cameron Webster.

Dallas Wiebe

is a Cincinnati writer and editor whose fiction and poetry are widely published. He is the author of a novel, Skyblue the Badass, (Doubleday, 1969), and a book of short stories, The Transparent Eye-Ball and Other Stories (Burning Deck Press, 1982). He has won the Aga Khan Fiction Prize from the PARIS REVIEW and has been included in a Pushcart Prize anthology (Vol. IV.)

"To My Valentine" and "The University Poet," reprinted by permission from OUTLAW II. "Down by the Salley Gardens" and "My Love is Like," © 1983 Dallas Wiebe.

David Young

lives in Oberlin where he co-edits FIELD with Stuart Friebert. Several collections of his poems have been published, the most recent of which are The Names of a Hare in English, and Worklights. In addition to an OAC fellowship, he has received a writing fellowship from the National Endowment for the Arts.

"Elegy in the Form of an Invitation," PLOUGHSHARES, © 1982 David Young.

Set in Rockwell typeface by the Writer's Center, Bethesda, Maryland;
Printed on 60 lb. Glatfelter text by Malloy Lithographing, Inc.,
Ann Arbor, Michigan.